THE CHALLENGE OF THE NORTH

JAMES HENDRYX

1st WORLD
LIBRARY
Literary Society

The Challenge of the North

James Hendryx

© 1st World Library, 2007
PO Box 2211
Fairfield, IA 52556
www.1stworldlibrary.com
First Edition

LCCN: 2007934153

Softcover ISBN: 978-1-4218-9653-3
Hardcover ISBN: 978-1-4218-9753-0
eBook ISBN: 978-1-4218-9553-6

Purchase *"The Challenge of the North"*
as a traditional bound book at:
www.1stWorldLibrary.com/purchase.asp?ISBN=978-1-4218-9653-3

1st World Library is a literary, educational organization
dedicated to:

- Creating a free internet library of downloadable ebooks

- Hosting writing competitions and offering book publishing
scholarships.

Interested in more 1st World Library books? contact:
literacy@1stworldlibrary.com
Check us out at: www.1stworldlibrary.com

1ˢᵗ World Library Literary Society

Giving Back to the World

"If you want to work on the core problem, it's early school literacy."

- James Barksdale, former CEO of Netscape

"No skill is more crucial to the future of a child, or to a democratic and prosperous society, than literacy."

- Los Angeles Times

"Literacy... means far more than learning how to read and write... The aim is to transmit... knowledge and promote social participation."

- UNESCO

"Literacy is not a luxury, it is a right and a responsibility. If our world is to meet the challenges of the twenty-first century we must harness the energy and creativity of all our citizens."

- President Bill Clinton

"Parents should be encouraged to read to their children, and teachers should be equipped with all available techniques for teaching literacy, so the varying needs and capacities of individual kids can be taken into account."

- Hugh Mackay

I

Oskar Hedin, head of the fur department of old John McNabb's big store, looked up from his scrutiny of the Russian sable coat spread upon a table before him, and encountered the twinkling eyes of old John himself.

"It's a shame to keep this coat here—and that natural black fox piece, too. Who is there in Terrace City that's got thirty thousand dollars to spend for a fur coat, or twenty thousand for a fox fur?"

Old John grinned. "Mrs. Orcutt bought one, didn't she?"

"Yes, but she bought it down in New York—"

"An' paid thirty-five thousand for a coat that runs half a dozen shades lighter, an' is topped an' pointed to bring it up to the best it's got. Did I ever tell ye the story of Mrs. Orcutt's coat?"

"No."

"It goes back quite a ways—the left-handed love me an' Fred Orcutt has for one another. We speak neighborly on the street, an' for years we've played on opposite sides of a ball-a-hole foursome at the Country Club, but either of us would sooner lose a hundred dollars than pay the other a golf ball.

"It come about in a business way, an' in a business way it's kept on. Not a dollar of McNabb money passes through the hands of Orcutt's Wolverine Bank—an' he could have had it all, an' he knows it.

"As ye know, I started out, a lad, with the Hudson's Bay Company, an' I'd got to be a factor when an old uncle of my mother's in Scotlan' died an' left me a matter of twenty thousand pounds sterling. When I got the money I quit the Company an' drifted around a bit until finally I bought up a big tract of Michigan pine. There wasn't any Terrace City then. I located a sawmill here at the mouth of the river an' it was known as McNabb's Landin'.

"D'ye see those docks? I built 'em, an' I've seen the time when they was two steamers warped along each side of 'em, an' one acrost the end, an' a half a dozen more anchored in the harbor waitin' to haul McNabb's lumber. The van stood on this spot in the sawmill days, an' when it got too small I built a wooden store. Folks began driftin' in. They changed the name from McNabb's Landin' to Terrace City, an' I turned a many a good dollar for buildin' sites.

"The second summer brought Fred Orcutt, an' I practically give him the best lot of the whole outfit to build his bank on. The town outgrew the wooden store an' I built this one, addin' the annex later, an' I ripped out the old dam an' put in a concrete dam an' a power plant that furnished light an' power for all Terrace City. Money was comin' in fast an' I invested it here an' there—Michigan, an' Minnesota, an' Winconsin pine, an' the Lord knows what not. Then come the panic, an' I found out almost over night that I was land poor. I needed cash, or credit at the bank, or I had to take a big loss. I went to see Fred Orcutt—I banked with him, those days, an' he knew the fix I was in. Yes, the bank would be glad to accommodate me all right; if you could of been there an' heard Fred Orcutt lay down his terms you'd know just how damn glad they'd of been to accommodate me. It kind of stunned me at first, an' then I saw red—the man I'd befriended in more ways than one, just layin' back till he had me in his clutches! Well, I lit out an' told him just what I thought of him—an' he got it in log camp English. It never fazed him. He just sat there leanin' back in his chair, bringin' the points of his fingers together an' drawin' 'em apart again, an' lookin' me square in the face with them pale blue fishy eyes of his. When I'd used up all the oaths an' epithets in common use, an' some new ones, an' had to quit, he says, in the same cold, even voice that he'd used in layin' down his terms, he says, 'You're a little excited now, John, and I'll not hold it against you. Just drop in sometime to-morrow or next day and we'll fix up the papers.'"

"I walked out of the bank with a wild scheme in my head of going to Detroit or Chicago for the money. But I knew it was no use—and so did Orcutt. He thought he had me right where he wanted me—an' so did I. Meanwhile, an' about six months previous, a young fellow named Charlie Bronson— president of the First National now—had opened up a little seven-by-nine bank in a tin-covered wooden shack that I'd passed a dozen times a day an' hadn't even looked into. I'd met Bronson once or twice, but hadn't paid no attention to him, an' as I was headin' back for the store, he stood in his doorway. 'Good mornin' Mr. McNabb,' he says. I don't think I'd of took the trouble to answer him, but just then his bank sign caught my eye. It was painted in black letters an' stuck out over the sidewalk. I stopped an' looked past him through the open door where his bookkeeper-payin'-an'-receivin'- teller-cashier, an' general factotum was busy behind the cheap grill. Then I looked at Bronson an' the only thing I noticed was that his eyes was brown, an' he was smilin'.

'Young man,' I says, 'have you got any money in that sardine can?'

"'Quite a lot,' he answers with a grin. 'More than I wish I had.'"

"'You got a hundred thousand?' I asks—it was more than I needed, but I thought I'd make it big enough to scare him."

"'More than that,' he answers, without battin' an eye. 'But— what's the matter with the Wolverine?'"

"'The Wolverine?' I busted out. 'Young man, if I was to tell you what I think of the Wolverine here on the street, I'd be arrested before I'd got good an' started.'"

"'Better come inside, then,' he grins, an' I followed him into a little box of a private office. 'Of course,' I says later, when I'd told him what I wanted, 'most of my collateral is pine timber, an' I suppose, as Orcutt says, it's depreciated—'"

"'Depreciated?' he asks. 'Why has it depreciated? It's all standin' on end, ain't it?' he says. An' it ain't gettin' no smaller, is it? An' they're layin' down the pine a damn sight faster than God Almighty can grow it, ain't they?' An' when I admitted that such was the facts, he laughed. 'Well then, we'll just go over your reports an' estimates, an' I don't think we'll have any trouble about doin' business.'"

"An we never have had no trouble, an' we've been doin' business every day since."

"But the coat?" reminded Hedin, after an interval of several minutes.

"I'm coming to that. Orcutt ain't human, but his wife is.

When he found out I'd slipped out of his clutches an' swung all my business over to Bronson's bank he never by so much as a word or a look let on that he even noticed it. They still have an account at the store; they can't help it, because no other store in Terrace City keeps the stock we do. But Mrs. Orcutt does all her real shoppin' in New York or Chicago."

II

Oskar Hedin loved fur, and the romance of fur. From his earliest recollection he had loved it as he had curled up and listened to the stories of his father, a great upstanding Viking of a sailor man, who year after year had forced his little vessel into the far North where he traded with the natives, and who had lost his life in the ice floes of the frozen sea while sailing with Nordenskjold.

Furs were to Hedin an obsession; they spoke a language he knew. He hated the grosser furs, as he loved the finer. He despised the trade tricks and spurious trade names by which the flimsiest of furs are foisted upon the gullible purchasers of "seal," "sable," "black fox," "ermine," and "beaver." He prided himself that no misnamed fur had ever passed over his counter, and in this he was backed up by his employer. The cheaper furs were there, but they sold under their true names and upon their merits.

In the social democracy of the town of twenty thousand people Oskar Hedin had earned a definite place. After graduating from the local high school he had entered the employ of McNabb, and within a very few years had been promoted to head his department. At the Country Club he could be depended upon to qualify with the first flight in the annual golf tournament, and the "dope" was all upset when he did not play in the finals on the courts. He lived at the city's only "family hotel," drove his own modest car, and religiously spent his Sundays on the trout streams.

Hedin picked up the coat and reverently deposited it in the fur safe. "It's a coat fit for a queen," he decided as he closed and locked the door. And Jean was the one woman in the world to wear it. Jean with the red blood coursing through her veins, her glow of health, and the sparkle of her eyes— McNabb's own daughter. "And, yet, I can't suggest it because—" Hedin muttered aloud and scowled at the floor. "I'd have asked her before this," he went on, "if that Wentworth hadn't butted in. Who knows anything about him, anyway? I'll ask her this afternoon." He stopped abruptly and smiled into the eyes of the girl who was hurrying toward him down the aisle.

"Oh, Oskar, I've just got a minute. I stopped in to remind you that this is Saturday, and we're going tobogganing this afternoon, and I've asked Mr. Wentworth and some of the crowd, and there'll be four or five toboggans, and it will be no end jolly. And this is my birthday, and you're a dear to think of it and send me all those flowers, and I'm going to wear 'em to-night. Listen, Elsie Campbell is giving a dinner for me this evening and of course you're not invited because it's just too funny the way she has snubbed you lately, and there's a show in town and after dinner we're going. Of course it won't be any good, but she's making a theatre party of it, and it sounds grand anyway. And I must hurry along now because I must remind Dad that he promised me a fur coat the day I was twenty-one, and I'll be back after a while and you can help me pick it out. Good-by, see you later!" And she was gone, leaving Hedin gazing after her with a smile as he strove to digest the jumble of uncorrelated information of which she had unburdened herself. "Wentworth, and some of the crowd! Oh, it will be jolly, all right—damn Wentworth!"

Old John McNabb looked up from his papers as his daughter burst into his private office and, rushing to his side, planted a kiss squarely upon the top of his bald head. "I came in to tell you I'm twenty-one to-day," she announced.

"Well, well, so ye are! Ye come into the world on the first of March, true to the old sayin', an' ye've be'n boisterous ever since. Twenty-one years old, an' tell me now, what have ye ever accomplished? When I was your age I'd be'n livin' in the bush north of 60 for two years, an' could do my fifty miles on snowshoes an' carry a pack."

"Maybe I can't do fifty miles a day on snowshoes, and I'm sure it isn't my fault I don't live north of 60. But I'm in a hurry; I promised to help Mr. Wentworth pick out a toboggan cap. I stopped in to remind you that you promised me a fur coat on my twenty-first birthday."

The old man regarded her thoughtfully. "So I did, so I did," he repeated absently. "This Wentworth, now—he's been kickin' around an uncommon lot, lately. Tell me again, who is he? What does he do for a livin'?"

"Why, he's a civil engineer—hydraulic work is his specialty. He has been employed by some company that intended to put in a power plant of some kind on Nettle River, and either the company broke up, or they found the plan was not feasible, or something, and they abandoned it. So Mr. Wentworth isn't doing anything, at present. But he is a fine fellow—so jolly, and so good looking, and he has a wonderful war record. He was with the engineers in Russia."

"U-m-m, where d'ye get hold of his war record?"

"Why—why—he—he has told us about the things they did—his company."

"Um—hum," Old John was stroking his nose.

"But, if he's civil engineer, an' out of a job, you might tell him to stop in a minute—after he gets the right color of a toboggan cap picked out."

III

When the door closed behind the girl old John readjusted his nose glasses and leaned back in his chair. "A clever engineer he is, beyond a doubt," he mused. "For I kept my eye on him while he was layin' out Orcutt's Nettle River project. If he'd made a botch of the job 'twould have saved me offerin' my plant to the city. But he has the look of a man ye couldn't trust in the dark—an' 'twould be clever engineerin' to marry a million. I'll set him a job that'll show the stuff that's in him. If he's a crook, I'll give him the chance to prove it." Reaching into a pigeon-hole of his desk, McNabb withdrew a thick packet of papers and removed the rubber band.

A few moments later Jean entered, the office followed by a rather well set up young man, whose tiny mustache was chopped square, like a miniature section of box hedge. "This is Mr. Wentworth, Dad," introduced the girl. "And now I'll leave you two men, because Oskar has promised to help me pick out a coat, and it's after ten o'clock. And, by the way, Dad, what kind of a coat shall I get? I want a good one."

"I'll warrant ye do! Well, just you tell Oskar to let you pick out a pony, or a crummer, or a baum marten, or a squirrel. They're all good."

As the door closed behind his daughter, old John McNabb

James Hendryx

motioned the younger man to a chair. "My daughter tells me you're an engineer," he began.

"Yes, sir, temporarily unemployed."

"Come up here on the Nettle River project, I hear. What's the matter? Couldn't you dam the river?"

"Oh, yes. The Nettle River presents no serious engineering problem. I spent four months on the ground and reported it favorably, and then all of a sudden, I was informed that the project had been abandoned, at least for the present. The trouble, I presume, was in the financing. It certainly was not because of any physical obstacles."

"What was the idea in building the dam in the first place?"

"Why, for power purposes. I believe it was their intention to induce manufacturing enterprises to locate in Terrace City, and to furnish them electric power at a low rate—"

"An' underbid me on the lightin' contract—an' then unload onto the city at a big profit."

Wentworth smiled. "I was not advised as to the financial end of it. I suppose, though, that that would have been the logical procedure."

Old John chuckled. "You're right, it would, with Fred Orcutt mixed up in it. But they didn't catch me nappin', an' I slipped the word to the city dads that I'd sell out to 'em, lock, stock, an' barrel, at a figure that would have meant a loss to Orcutt's crowd to meet. So I'm the one that busted the Nettle River bubble, an' seein' I knocked ye out of a job, it's no more than fair I should offer ye another."

"Why, thank you—"

"Don't thank me yet," interrupted McNabb. "Ye may not care to tackle it. It's a man's size job, in a man's country. Part of it's the same kind of work you've been doin' here—locatin' a dam to furnish power to run a pulp mill. Then you'll have to check up the land covered by that batch of options, an' explore a couple of rivers, an' locate more pulpwood, an' get options on it. An' lay out a road to the railway. It's in Canada, in the Gods Lake Country, three hundred miles north of the railhead."

"How soon would you expect me to start?"

"Monday wouldn't be none too soon; to-morrow would be better. It's this way. I've got options on better than half a million acres of pulpwood lyin' between Hayes River an' the Shamattawa. Ten years ago I cut the last of my pine, an' I got out my pencil an' begun to figure how I could keep in the woods. I pig-ironed a little—got out hardwood for the wooden specialty factories to cut up into spools, an' clothes-pins, an' oval dishes an' whatnot—an' then I turned my attention to the pulpwood. I figured it wouldn't be long before the papermills would be hollerin' for raw materials the way they was turnin' out the paper, so I nosed around a bit an' bought options on pulpwood land here an' there. An' now's the time to get busy, with the big newspapers an' the magazines all howlin' for paper, an' all the mills workin' overtime."

"Do you mean that you're going to manufacture paper yourself—way up there? How do you expect to get your product to market?"

"Easy enough. Make the paper in the woods, an' float it a little better than a hundred miles to Hudson Bay in barges, or scows. You see, the Shamattawa runs into Hayes River, an' Hayes River empties into the Bay just across a spit of land from Port Nelson. And the railway from The Pas to Port Nelson is being pushed to completion. With the paper on the Bay, I can ship by rail or boat to the market."

"And you want to locate the mill on the Hayes River?"

"No; the Hayes runs too flat. Either on the upper Shamattawa, or on Gods River, which lies between the two, an' flows into the Shamattawa. There's plenty of water in either one, an' I think both or 'em have got fall enough. I want the mill where it will be easy to get the wood to it, an' at the same time, where we'll have a good head of water—an' it's got to be done quick. The options expire the first of August, an' I've nosed around an' found out there's no chance to renew 'em on decent terms. When you get the mill located, then you've got to slip down the river an' find out what kind of scows we'll need, an' lay out a road to the new Hudson Bay Railway that's headed for Port Nelson. We'll haul in the material an' save time. An' when you've finished that, you can make a survey of the pulpwood available outside our present holdin's."

"Quite a job, take it all in all."

"Yes—an' takin' it all in all, it'll take quite a man to fill it," retorted McNabb brusquely. "The man that puts this through won't never need to hunt another job, because this is only the beginnin' of the pulpwood game for me—" The telephone on the desk rang, and after a moment's conversation, McNabb arose and tossed the packet of papers into Wentworth's lap. "I've got to step out for a matter of ten or fifteen minutes," he said. "Here's the papers, an' a map of the country. Look 'em over, an' if you care to tackle it, let me know when I come back."

Alone in the office, Wentworth studied the map fully five minutes; then he read over the option contract. Suddenly, he straightened in his chair, and read the last clause of the contract carefully:

Be it further agreed that if the said John McNabb, or his authorized representative, does not demand fulfillment of the terms of this agreement, and accompany the said demand by tender of at least ten percent of the purchase price named herein, on or before noon of the first day of July, nineteen hundred and twenty-one, this agreement shall automatically become null and void in its entirety.

Be it further agreed between the said John McNabb, and the said Canadian Wild Lands Company, Ltd., that aforementioned demand and tender of payment shall be made at and in the store of that trading post of the Hudson's Bay Company, situated upon the north shore of Gods Lake, and known as Gods Lake Post.

Swiftly Wentworth stepped to the desk and, lifting the receiver from its hook, called a number. "Hello! Wolverine Bank? I want to speak with Mr. Orcutt. Hello, Mr. Orcutt? This is Wentworth—No, I don't want any money. Listen, I must see you at once. I'm on the trail of something big, and I need you to help swing it. There's a million in it—can't say more now. What? One o'clock at the bank? Right, I'll be there. Good-by."

A few moments later McNabb entered the office. "Well, did you look the proposition over? Ye see by the map how we can get the paper to the Bay. What d'ye say? Take it, or leave it?"

"I'll take it," answered Wentworth.

"An' ye'll start to-morrow?"

"Why—it's pretty short notice—but—yes, I'll start to-morrow."

Old John McNabb drew a check which he handed to Wentworth.

"Expenses, an' a month's advance salary," grunted the older man.

"And when do you want a report on the mill site?"

"As soon after the ice goes out as you can make it."

"And you will be up during the summer?"

"Some time in July—I've got to be there on the first of August to close that option. Take those location papers with ye. Ye'll need them, an' the map—I have another copy in the vault at the bank. I'll bring 'em up when I come, so if somethin' comes up so you couldn't be at the post on the first of August, it won't hold up the deal. Run along now, I must catch the 11:45 train for Grand Rapids—see you in July."

IV

Upstairs in the fur department Oskar Hedin paused in the act of returning some fox pieces to their place, and greeted the girl who had halted before the tall pier glass to readjust her hat and push a refractory strand of hair into place. "Back again?" he smiled. "And now for the coat!"

"Now for the coat," she repeated. "What kind of a coat do I want, Oskar? I want to try on lots of them. I don't know a thing in the world about furs. All I know is that I've seen some I liked, and some that I didn't care much for."

For half an hour Jean tried on coats, until her choice had narrowed down to a handsome dark baum marten, and a shimmery gray squirrel.

"I think they're both lovely, and I can't quite make up my mind," she said at last, in a tone of mock despair. "It's worse than picking out toboggan caps. I just helped Mr. Wentworth select one—and, oh, by the way, I believe dad is going to find a place for him."

"For who?" asked Hedin, and Jean noticed tiny wrinkles gather between his eyes.

"Why, for Mr. Wentworth, of course. You see, I told dad that he'd just lost his position with that old Nettle River thing they were trying to put through, and Dad said if he was a civil engineer, and out of a job, to tell him to drop in and see him, so I took him in and introduced him and I guess they're still talking."

"Humph," grunted Hedin.

"You don't need to be so grumpy about it. Mr. Wentworth is awfully nice, and all the girls are crazy about him."

"I don't think that gives you any call to rave much over him when it was Fred Orcutt that brought him here, and he brought him for no other purpose than to knife your father," replied Hedin dryly.

Jean laughed. "You take Dad too seriously. He really believes Mr. Orcutt has it in for him, and he sees an ulterior motive in everything he does in a business way. But, really, the Orcutts are all right. There was some business deal, years and years ago, in which Dad fancied Mr. Orcutt tried to get the best of him, and he has never forgotten it. You see, Dad is the dearest thing that ever lived, but he is sort of crusty, and it isn't everybody that knows how to take him. Why, Mr. and Mrs. Orcutt are going to be at dinner this evening, and are going to the theatre, too. They know it is my birthday party, so that doesn't look as though they were such fierce enemies of the McNabbs, does it?

"Let's get back to the subject of coats. This squirrel is beautiful, but I believe I like the dark fur the better. I think I'll try that marten again."

Hedin was thinking rapidly. He had known from the first that the darker fur was the fur for her, yet he had refrained from making any direct suggestion.

"Just a moment, please," he said. "Won't you button that coat once more, I want to get an artificial light effect." As he spoke, he moved toward the windows and drew the shades. Returning in the gloom, he reached swiftly into the fur safe and withdrew the Russian sable coat which he deftly deposited on top of the marten coat that lay with several others upon a nearby table. As the girl turned from the glass, he switched on the light.

"All right," he said, a moment later. "If you care to try on the marten again, we'll see how that shows up under the artificial." Deftly he lifted the squirrel from her shoulders, and, picking up the Russian sable, held it while she slipped her arms into the sleeves. As she buttoned it, he stepped back, and viewed the result through critically puckered eyes. With an effort he refrained from voicing his enchantment with the living picture before him. Old John was right—it was a coat fit for a queen!

"I like this one best. I'll take it."

Hedin agreed. "I think you have chosen wisely," he answered, adding, as she started to loosen the garment at the throat, "Just a minute—the set of the collar in the back—" He stepped behind her, raised the collar a trifle with his fingers, smoothed it into place, and stepped aside to note the effect. "Just a trifle low," he said, "but it's too late to have it altered to-day."

"Oh, bother! I think the set is all right. Who would ever notice it? Let it go."

Hedin smiled. "You can wear it to-night, all right, but you must promise me to send it down the first thing Monday morning for the alteration.

"I will bring it to the house this afternoon."

A sudden caprice seized her. "Why, I think I'll wear it!" she answered. "Just help me on with it, Oskar. And thank you so much for helping me select it. Here comes Mr. Wentworth, now. I wonder whether he will like it. I'm crazy about it. What kind of a marten did you say it is? Everybody will be asking me, and I want to be able to tell them what my own coat is."

"Baum marten," answered Hedin stiffly, heartily wishing the coat safe in its accustomed place. In vain he regretted the wild impulse that had led him to substitute the sable coat for the marten. The impulse had come when the girl told him that Mrs. Orcutt was to be one of the theatre party. The plan had flashed upon him with overwhelming brilliance. He knew that Jean would in all probability never notice that the coat was not a marten. And he knew that Mrs. Orcutt most certainly would, for McNabb had once publicly compared it with her coat, much to the New York coat's detriment and Mrs. Orcutt's humiliation. It was not altogether loyalty for his employer that led him to plot the woman an uncomfortable evening, for he owed her a grudge on his own account. Ever since the coming of Wentworth, whom she had taken under her special patronage, Hedin had been studiously omitted from her scheme of social activities—and Jean McNabb had been as studiously included. He knew that McNabb was leaving town to be gone until the following evening, and that the chance of his seeing the garment was exceedingly small, and he had invented the fiction of the low collar in order to get the coat back on Monday morning when he would, of course, substitute the baum marten and return the sable to its safe. But now he felt vaguely uneasy.

Hedin saw that Wentworth was staring at the coat with a swiftly appraising eye. "It's a baum marten," Jean went on.

"It took me a long time to choose between this and a squirrel. There was one that was a luscious gray, but I like this better—don't you?"

Wentworth nodded. "I certainly do," he agreed. "And I do not believe it would have taken me long to decide between that and a squirrel." He turned to Hedin. "What do you think, Mr.—ah—Haywood? That the choice was a wise one? This is certainly a handsome—er—what did you say it is?"

"Baum marten," snapped Hedin, with scarcely a glance at the questioner, as he turned and began to replace the coats that lay upon the table. Wentworth watched Hedin return the baum marten to its place, and Jean stepped swiftly to Hedin's side.

As she spoke, he saw that her eyes were flashing angrily.

"If your surly mood doesn't change," she whispered, "you will not add much to the enjoyment of our coasting party."

"I shall neither add to, nor detract from it," answered Hedin, meeting her gaze squarely. "Please don't wait for me. I find that I shall not be able to attend."

V

The United States Government formally entered the world war in April, and the following month Ross Wentworth had been graduated from a technical college, and through the auspices of an influential relative was commissioned a captain of engineers, and assigned to duty in one of the larger cantonments. In due course of events he was sent overseas, and was attached to the forces operating in northern Russia. During the sixteen months of his service in the land of the erstwhile Czar, he acquired a fund of military terms, both official and slang. Also he built and maintained in a state of inutility, nine and one-half miles of military swamp road, over which no gun nor detachment of troops ever passed. The abrupt termination of hostilities caught him with a formidable and inexplicable discrepancy of company funds—which discrepancy was promptly and liberally met by the aforementioned relative. Whereupon, Captain Wentworth was honorably discharged from the service of his country.

For many months after his discharge he lived by his wits and looks, but when this grew unproductive of ready cash, he decided to seek employment in his accredited vocation.

This decision he arrived at while sojourning in the home of a wealthy fruit-grower who was interested in the Nettle River project, and who furnished him a letter of recommendation to Orcutt, who promptly employed him. Thereafter all went well until McNabb's ultimatum brought the Nettle River project to as sudden a termination as the armistice had brought the war. Whereupon Wentworth found himself in the uncomfortable predicament of having no available assets and many pressing liabilities, incurred in the course of his endeavor to win the good graces of the wealthy Jean McNabb.

While scarcely knowing Hedin, Wentworth recognized him as a possible rival. He, himself, was no connoisseur of fur, but at least he knew a Russian sable when he saw one, and as he preceded Jean down the aisle, his brain worked rapidly.

By the time he reached the street, a daring scheme was half-formed in his brain—a scheme which, if successful, would work the utter ruin of Hedin, and leave him a clear field with the girl. At the first corner he excused himself.

Hardly was the girl's back turned when Wentworth dodged around the corner and entered McNabb's store by another door just in time to see old John rush from the building, bag in hand, and hurry down the street in the direction of the station.

McNabb's was the only big store in Terrace City, and being a department store, it kept city hours, so while on Saturday evenings all the other stores remained open for business until a late hour, McNabb's closed at noon. Passing unnoticed down the aisle, Wentworth's eyes darted here and there in search of a place of concealment, until at length he took up a position close beside McNabb's private office, the door of which, he noted with satisfaction, stood slightly ajar.

Watching his opportunity, Wentworth slipped unnoticed into

the private office, closed the door softly behind him, and sank comfortably into McNabb's desk chair.

A gong sounded, and was repeated, dimly, upon the floors above. Wentworth could hear the tramp of feet in the aisles as the clerks poured from the building through a door that gave on to a side street. In a few minutes the rush was over, and then they came scatteringly, singly, and by twos and threes. He could hear the opening of the door, and the click of the lock as it closed behind them. The footsteps ceased. He drew his watch and waited. Noises from the street reached him, sounding far off and muffled, but the store was silent as a tomb. Twelve minutes ticked away. A footstep sounded. Wentworth could trace it descending the stairs, and walking the length of an aisle. Followed the sound of the opening door, and the click of the latch. Some belated department head, he thought. Possibly Hedin, himself—and he grinned at the thought.

In the silence of the great building Wentworth suddenly realized that he was nervous. It was all well enough to plan a thing, but the carrying out of the plan was quite another matter. He took a silent turn or two the length of the office, his footsteps making no sound upon the soft carpet. He waited twenty minutes and, hearing no sound, closed his watch and dabbed at his forehead with the handkerchief which he drew from his sleeve. Turning the knob, he stepped out upon the uncarpeted floor. The sound of his footsteps upon the hardwood seemed to reverberate through the whole building. He walked a few steps on tiptoe, and then decided that in case anyone should see him, the tiptoeing would look furtive. So he walked to the foot of the stairway, his footsteps sounding in his ears like the ring of a hammer on an anvil. As he ascended the stairs he called out, "Hey, isn't there any one here? I am locked in, and can't get out! Hello! Someone show me the way out!"

Swiftly he ascended to the third floor and crossed to the fur case. Silently he slid back the door and lifted the baum marten coat from its place, and stepping to a counter upon which was fixed a huge roll of wrapping paper, he proceeded to make the coat into a package. This done, he hastened toward the stairway with the package under his arm. Down the stairs he flew, taking them two and three at a time, down the next flight, and across the floor, until he brought up panting at the door with the spring lock by which the employees had left the building.

Thought of material gain had not until this point entered into the scheme. He had merely plotted the undoing of a rival, but at the sudden realization of his status in the eyes of the world, a new thought struck him. "If I can get away with it— why not? A Russian sable! Why, it's worth *thousands*!"

It took a concentrated effort to open the door a tiny crack and peer through. Swiftly opening the door, Wentworth stepped onto the sidewalk, closed the door behind him, and clutching his package tightly, hurried down the street. He had entirely gained his composure by the time he reached his hotel, and hastening to his room, placed the package in his trunk and turned the key. He glanced at his watch. It lacked three minutes of one, and remembering his appointment with Orcutt, he hastened to the Wolverine Bank.

VI

Orcutt greeted his caller without enthusiasm. For despite the assurance over the telephone that Wentworth wanted no money, he felt that he was in for a touch.

The younger man was quick to note the attitude, and hastened to dispel it. "In the first place, Mr. Orcutt, I am going to ask you to cash a check for three thousand dollars, but—"

"Three thousand!" exclaimed Orcutt, his eyes narrowing. "Whose check is it?"

"John McNabb's."

"John McNabb's!" A look of suspicion flashed into his eyes.

"Yes—isn't it good?"

"Good! Hell—yes, of course it's good! But what are you doing with McNabb's check for three thousand?"

Reaching into his pocket, Wentworth drew out the packet of papers and held it in his hand. "Eight or ten years ago McNabb bought options on a half million acres of pulp-wood lying between two certain rivers. He sent for me—said he heard I was out of a job, and that as he was the one that was responsible for my losing out, it was only fair that he should offer me another. Then he went on to outline the whole proposition, told me the options expired on August first; then he was called out of the office for a minute and asked me to look over the maps and papers and let him know if I wanted to tackle it or not.

"In going over the contract, I found that the options expire on July first, instead of August first, as he said. It was then I called you up, for the whole scheme hit me like a flash. Don't you see it? If I worked for him, I'd draw a salary, and a good one—and nothing more. But if I should interest sufficient capital to step in on the first day of July when those options expire, and buy up the whole tract, where would McNabb be?"

Orcutt tapped thoughtfully upon his desk pad with the tip of his pencil. "I wonder," he muttered aloud, more to himself than to Wentworth, "I wonder if John has made a slip at last?"

"That is just what he has done! And he is so cocksure of his ground that he didn't even glance at the papers to refresh his memory—I doubt if he has looked at them since he made the deal."

The banker eyed the younger man shrewdly. "And in case I should interest myself in the proposition to the extent of organizing the capital to swing the deal, what would you expect out of it?"

"A share in the business, and a salary of ten thousand a year."

"You don't want much!" exclaimed Orcutt.

"Not any more than you could well afford to give me. You don't realize what a big thing this is—it's going to take a lot of capital to swing it."

"About how much?"

"You'll have to get your figures on the paper mill from someone that knows more about it than I do. The pulp-wood will cost, I imagine, somewhere between six and ten dollars an acre. McNabb's options call for purchase at five dollars, and he told me he could not renew at that figure. But even at ten dollars, there is a mint in it. You will have to pay down ten percent of the purchase price in cash."

Orcutt whistled. "Ten percent of the purchase price, at say, ten dollars, would be half a million. Besides the cost of the mill and the interest on four million and a half!"

"It is a big proposition," agreed Wentworth. "If it is too big for you to handle, I can find someone who will. I have a friend in Detroit whose father will jump at the chance. It isn't too big for McNabb."

"Who said anything about it being too big?" snapped Orcutt. "If McNabb could find the money, I can. But, mind you, I'm not going to spend a damned cent on the proposition until after McNabb's options have expired and we've got our hands on the pulp-wood. Mind you; you don't draw any advance money."

"Not a cent," agreed Wentworth. "But you'd better have the money right on hand on the first day of July; those options expire at noon, and we don't want any delay about getting hold of the property. And, by the way, I want a written contract—make my share a ten percent interest in the business."

After some demurring on the part of Orcutt, he called a stenographer and drew a contract, which he duly signed and handed to Wentworth, who thrust it into his pocket with the packet of papers.

"Let's see those papers of McNabb's," said Orcutt.

Wentworth smiled. "That is hardly necessary, do you think? I will vouch for the date—and the location need not concern you at present. All you need to know is that at noon on the first day of July, you, or your legal representative, must be at the Gods Lake post of the Hudson's Bay Company, with a half million dollars in cash, or its equivalent—and you'd better have all your arrangements made in advance, and allow plenty of time to get there."

VII

On the whole the afternoon was a disappointing one for Jean McNabb. She had been deeply hurt by Hedin's curt refusal to attend the coasting party, and Wentworth had proved a very luke-warm cavalier. She had started out to be extremely vivacious so all might see that the absence of Hedin was a matter of no concern, but Wentworth's preoccupied manner soon dampened her ardor, until for her the coasting party became a monotonous affair.

She breathed a sigh of relief when it was over, and after a walk, during which neither ventured a word, she parted from Wentworth at the gate and rushed to her room. She was furious with Hedin, furious with Wentworth, and furious with herself for being furious.

When he parted from Jean McNabb after the coasting party, Wentworth proceeded to the railway station, where he purchased his ticket and arranged with a truckman to call for his trunk at exactly eight o'clock. Hastening to the hotel, he dressed for dinner.

This accomplished, he carefully locked his door, removed the coat from his trunk, concealed it within the folds of his own overcoat, and sat down to smoke a cigarette as he went over, step by step, his hastily conceived plan. When the hands of his watch indicated that he would be precisely fifteen minutes late, he left the hotel, carrying the overcoat upon his arm.

The street into which he turned was deserted, and proceeding to a point opposite the Campbell residence, he stepped behind a huge maple tree and surveyed the brilliantly lighted house across the way.

"They're late getting started. I hope they are not waiting on my account," he grinned, and drew closer into the shadow of the trees as a lone pedestrian passed along the opposite sidewalk. Faintly to his ears came the sound of laughter, and then there was a general exodus toward the dining room. With a sigh of relief, Wentworth crossed the street, rang the doorbell, and was admitted.

"That you, Captain Wentworth?" called his hostess. "We waited for you until just this minute."

"Awfully sorry to be late—detestable thing to do—going away in the morning—thousand-and-one things to attend to—be down in a moment to offer humble apology."

Swiftly and silently Wentworth removed the coat from within his own, crossed the hall, substituted the baum marten for the Russian sable, and reentered the gentlemen's dressing room, where it was but the work of a moment to conceal the garment within the folds of his coat. Then he descended the stairs, entered the dining room, and seated himself in the vacant chair beside Jean McNabb.

The dinner went as dinners do and was brought to a rather abrupt termination by someone's discovery that it lacked but five minutes to eight. As the guests rose from the table Wentworth gave a startled exclamation.

"In my haste in dressing I forgot my pocketbook. I distinctly recollect removing it from my pocket and tossing it upon the bed, and there I must have left it." He turned to Elsie Campbell. "I hope you will pardon me if I hurry away but really, that pocketbook contains a rather large sum—expense money you know—and, I am almost certain that I neglected to lock my room. I will join you at the door of the theatre; I can easily reach there before you, if I hurry."

A moment later he rushed from the house with his overcoat upon his arm, and hurried to the hotel where, lifting the tray of his trunk, he deposited the sable coat, replaced the tray, locked and strapped the trunk, and finished just in time to respond to the knock of the truckman. Five minutes later he was waiting at the theatre for the others, who appeared just before the rise of the curtain on the first act.

VIII

When Oskar Hedin left the store at the closing hour, he went directly to his hotel, bolted a hasty luncheon, slipped into outdoor togs and a half hour later was silently threading an old log-trail that bit deep into the jack-pines. Mile after mile he glided smoothly along that silent winding white lane, his skis making no sound in the soft, deep snow.

Just beyond a swamp, in the centre of a wide clearing, surrounded upon three sides by the encroaching jack-pines and poplars, and upon the fourth by a broad bend of the river, Hedin removed his skis and seated himself upon a rotting log of a tumbled-down cabin, there to think.

So, that's why she wanted a new coat? She was going out for the evening with Wentworth. And she invited Wentworth to go tobogganing, on this particular afternoon of all others, when he had intended to whisper in her ear, as the toboggan flew down the steep grade, the thing that had been uppermost in his mind for a year. And she had asked her father to give him a job. Of course, what could be simpler? A man can manage to exist, somehow, without a job—but with two a job is essential.

He laughed, a short, hard laugh that ended in a sneer. Well, he had been a fool—that's all. He had served her purpose, had been the poor dupe upon whom she had practised her wiles, a plaything, to be lightly tossed aside for a new toy. Some day, too late perhaps, she would see her mistake, and then she would suffer, even as he was suffering now—but, no, to suffer one must first love, and woman had not the capacity to love. "To hell with them!" he cried aloud. "To hell with my tame job! And to hell with Terrace City, and with the civilization that calls a man from the wild places and sets him to selling women baubles to deck themselves out in."

The jack-pine shadows reached far into the clearing as Oskar fastened on his skis and headed back along the tote-road. It was not too late—he was only twenty-five. He, too, would live like a man, would go into the North, and henceforth only the outlands should know him. He would resign Monday morning. The thought caused a pang of regret at parting with McNabb.

Darkness found him still upon the tote-road. He emerged from the jack-pines and paused at the long smooth hill, as was his wont, to look down upon the brilliant lights of Terrace City. His momentum carried him skimming across a flat meadow, and he slowed to a stand at the very end of the main street where, in the white glare of an arc light he removed his skis, and stepped onto the sidewalk.

Well, he would see her once more, arrayed in the coat of matched sable—and he would carry the picture with him to far places where the stars winked cold in the night sky.

Fully twenty minutes before time for the curtain Hedin was in his place, tenth row on the middle aisle, eagerly scanning the patrons as they were ushered to their seats. The theatre boasted only two boxes, set just above the stage level, and Elsie Campbell had engaged them both.

As time for the curtain to rise drew near, Hedin found himself fidgeting nervously. Had the theatre party been called off? The house was already well filled; surely there was no block of vacant seats that would accommodate a dinner party. Then, as he had about given up hope, he raised his eyes to a box just as Jean McNabb entered, followed closely by Wentworth. Hedin stared as if petrified, brushed his hand across his eyes as though to clear his vision of distorting film, and stared again. For Wentworth was lifting a coat from Jean's shoulders, but it was not a sable one. Seizing his hat and coat, Hedin rushed from the building, narrowly avoiding collision with an usher.

Without pausing to put on his coat, he dashed for the store and letting himself in, took the stairs three at a time. Upon the second flight, he met the night watchman who, recognizing him, allowed him to pass, but noting his evident agitation and unaccountable haste, silently and discreetly followed and took up a position where he could watch every move of the excited department head. Hastening to the fur safe, Hedin unlocked and threw it open. He switched on the light, and peered into the interior. The Russian sable coat was not in its accustomed place. And a hurried search of the safe showed that it was in no other place. Closing the door, he inspected the case that contained the less valuable furs, and it was but the work of a moment to discover that the baum marten coat was missing. Dumbfounded, he stared at the empty space where the coat should have been. His brief inspection in the theatre had told him this was the coat Jean McNabb was wearing—but where was the sable? He distinctly remembered replacing the marten with his own hands, and of seeing the girl pass down the aisle wearing the sable.

He sank into his chair and, leaning forward, buried his face in his arms upon his desk. He tried to think clearly, but found himself entirely incapable of thought. How did it happen? Where was the sable?

Calling the watchman, Hedin questioned him for half an hour, but learned nothing. He even made a personal inspection of every door and window in the store, and sent the watchman to the basement on a tour of similar inspection. When the man returned and reported nothing disturbed, Hedin left the store and proceeded directly to his room, where he spent a sleepless night in trying to solve the mystery.

After breakfast the following morning Jean McNabb sat before the little dressing table in her room when the doorbell rang, and the maid announced Mr. Hedin.

"Tell Mr. Hedin I can't see anyone this morning," she said, without looking up.

Again the maid tapped at the door, and entering, handed the girl a hastily scribbled leaf torn from a notebook. Jean read it at a glance, and her face flushed with swift anger. No salutation, only a few scrawled words: "Must see you at once. Purely matter of business—very important—about the coat."

Crossing to her desk the girl scribbled upon the reverse side of the paper. "Never talk business on Sunday. Coat will be at store as per agreement."

IX

On Monday morning old John McNabb entered his private office to find Hedin awaiting him. He glanced at the younger man inquiringly—"What ails ye, lad? Ye look like ye hadn't slept for a week."

"I haven't slept for two nights," answered Hedin. "There is no use beating around the bush. As a matter of fact, the Russian sable coat is missing, and I am to blame for it."

The old man stared incredulously. "Missin'!" he exclaimed. "An' you're to blame! What d'ye mean?"

Hastily, in as few words as possible, Hedin recited the facts as he knew them, while an angry flush mounted to the old man's face.

McNabb reached for the telephone and called a number. "Hello! Is that you, Jean? Come to the store at once, and bring your new fur coat—to my office. . . . What? No, that won't do, at all. Bring it yourself—I'm waitin'."

"I'll step outside while Jean—while Miss McNabb—"

"Ye'll stay where ye are!" snapped McNabb.

The older man turned to his desk, where for ten minutes he opened and closed drawers and rustled papers viciously. Then the door opened and Jean herself stepped into the room with the fur coat over her arm. "Well, Dad, here's the coat." She paused abruptly, glanced inquiringly at Hedin, nodded coolly, and continued, "Oskar said it needed a little tailoring, and that I was to bring it down this morning, but I didn't think there was any tearing hurry about it."

Her father took the garment, smoothed the fur with his hand, and asked casually, "Is this the coat ye wore from the store?"

"Why, of course it is."

"An' the one ye wore to the show?"

"Yes, yes," answered the girl impatiently. "I haven't so many fur coats that I would be apt to get them mixed."

McNabb ignored the impatience. "Ye've had no other coat in your possession since you selected this one?"

"No, I haven't. What's all this about?"

"Did Oskar tell you what kind of a coat you were gettin'?"

"Yes, a baum marten. Why, isn't it a baum marten?"

McNabb nodded. "Yes, it's a baum marten. Run along now. I just wanted to see which coat ye'd got. Here, take it along with ye. The tailor can wait."

With a puzzled glance at the two men, Jean took the coat, and with a toss of the head left the office.

McNabb turned to Hedin. "What have ye got to say now?

Did the girl tell the truth?"

"Absolutely."

"Then that was the coat she wore from the store?"

"No—but she thinks it was. She doesn't know the difference."

For a long time John McNabb spoke no word but sat staring at his desk, pecking at the blotter with his pencil. He prided himself upon his ability to pick men. He knew men, and in no small measure was this knowledge responsible for his success in dealing with men. He had been certain that Jean and Hedin would eventually marry, and secretly he longed for the day. He had watched Hedin for years and now, despite the improbability of the story, he believed it implicitly. And it was with a heavy heart that he had watched the studied coldness of each toward the other. McNabb was a man of snap decisions. He would teach these young fools a lesson, and at the same time find out which way the wind blew. With a clenching of his fists, he whirled abruptly upon Hedin.

"What did ye do with the coat?" he roared. "It'll go easier with ye if ye tell me!"

"What do you mean?" cried Hedin, white to the lips, meeting McNabb's gaze with a look of mingled surprise, pain, and anger.

"I mean just what I say. Ye've got the coat—where is it?"

Hedin felt suddenly weak and sick. He had expected McNabb's anger at his foolish whim, and knew that he deserved it—but that McNabb should accuse him of theft!

Sick at heart, he faltered his answer, and in his own ears his voice sounded strange, and dull, and unconvincing. "You think I—I stole it?"

"What else am I to think? What will the police think? What will the jury think when they hear your flimsy yarn—an' the straightforward evidence of my daughter? They'll think that the coat she wore to the show, an' that she still has, is the coat she wore from the store, an' that you've got the other. An' when Kranz tells of your midnight visit to the store, what'll they think then?" McNabb finished and, reaching for the telephone, called the police headquarters. A few minutes later the chief himself appeared, accompanied by the night watchman, Kranz, whose story of the nervous and agitated appearance of Hedin on his midnight visit to the store forged the strongest link in the chain of circumstantial evidence.

After the watchman had been dismissed, Hedin was subjected to a bullying at the hands of the burly officer that stopped just short of personal violence, and through it all he stubbornly maintained his innocence.

After another brief telephone conversation, the three visited the private room of the judge where, waiving a preliminary hearing, the prisoner was bound over to await the action of the grand jury, and his bail fixed at ten thousand dollars.

X

At the mouth of the alley that led from a side street to the rear of the jail, the policeman plucked at Hedin's sleeve, and turned in. Mechanically Hedin fell in beside him. Someone passed upon the street. "See who that was?" asked the officer maliciously, for he knew all the town gossip. Hedin scarcely heard the question. "It was McNabb's gal. Her throwin' you over fer this here Wentworth didn't give you no license to steal her old man's fur coat, all right—but maybe you ain't so onlucky, at that. Folks says she's all right—a little gay an' the like of that—but runnin' the streets at midnight, like she was a Saturday, with a guy that goes after 'em like Wentworth! Call it gay if they want to, but if it was anyone but old McNabb's daughter, they'd be callin' it somethin' else."

Smash! Hedin's fist drove with terrific force into the flappy jaw, and the big officer reeled, and crashed into the snow between a row of ash barrels, and a dilapidated board fence. The young man stared in surprise as he waited for the other to regain his feet. The officer's words had roused a sudden flash of fury, and with nerves already strained to the breaking point, he had struck. But the man, grotesquely sprawled behind the barrels, made no move.

Hedin glanced up and down the alley. It was empty. He was free! Swiftly he proceeded down the alley, passed the jail, and turned into the street. Here he slackened his pace, and walking leisurely to his hotel, hastily made up a light pack. Passing around to the rear, he took his skis from their place, walking to the edge of town, fastened them on, and was soon swallowed up in the jack-pines. For an hour he glided smoothly over the snow, and upon the edge of a balsam thicket sat down on a log to rest.

There were two courses open. Either he could return to Terrace City and face the charge against him as best he could, or he could keep going. It was only a few miles across country to Pipe Lake, where he could catch the P.M. for Detroit.

His thoughts turned abruptly from the problem of flight, and plunged into the problem of the missing coat. It was not conceivable that the garment had been destroyed; therefore it was still in existence. If in existence, somebody had it. Who? One by one, Hedin considered the personnel of the theatre party, and one by one he eliminated them until only Wentworth was left. Wentworth! If he could only prove it! He remembered that someone had casually remarked that morning at breakfast that Wentworth had gone North for old John McNabb. He had heard McNabb mention some pulp-wood lands in the North. Gods Lake, wasn't it? Why, Gods Lake post was old Dugald Murchison's post! Hedin remembered Murchison well. It was only last year he had spent a week as the guest of his old friend McNabb, and nearly every evening at dinner Hedin had sat at meat with them, and listened in fascination to the talk of the far outlands. He remembered the shrewd gray eyes of Murchison—eyes that bespoke wisdom, and justice tempered with mercy.

He smote his leg with his mittened fist. He would go North, straight to old Dugald Murchison, and he would tell him the whole story. Murchison would help him, and if Wentworth were innocent, then he, Hedin would return to Terrace City and give himself up. He would not be a fugitive from justice, for justice owed him the chance to prove his innocence.

Once his mind was made up, Hedin rose to his feet and slung the light pack to his back. Then he lowered the pack, and stood thinking. He would hit for Pipe Lake, but Hanson, the storekeeper at Pipe Lake, would recognize him. Tossing his pack aside, he scooped a hole in the snow, built a tiny fire of balsam twigs, and melted some water in his drinking cup. Then, setting a small hand mirror upon the log, he produced his razor and proceeded to shave off his mustache. This done, he grinned at himself in the mirror, as he reflected that Hanson had never seen him except in conventional clothing, and that he would never recognize him in mackinaw and larrigans, with his mustache gone.

Once more he stood up, kicked snow over his fire, swung the pack to his back, and started to skirt the swamp. Then suddenly he halted in his tracks. There was a mighty crackling of dry twigs close at hand, and a voice commanded gruffly, "Hands up!"

Instinctively Hedin elevated his hands as he stared into the muzzle of a revolver. Beyond the revolver he saw the grinning face of Mike Duffy, erstwhile lumberjack, then bootlegger, and now policeman; under the Hicks regime.

"Shaved her off, eh?" taunted the man. "Well, mebbe you'd 'a' fooled most folks, but you hain't fooled me none, special' as I be'n layin' in the brush watchin' you fer half an hour. You'd of got away from the rest of 'em too."

XI

Old John McNabb had not been long at his desk when the telephone bell rang and he picked up the receiver.

"Hello—who? Hicks? He—what? Where is he now? Got away! Well, you get him! Get him, or I'll get you! If he ain't back in jail to-day, off comes your buttons to-morrow—do you get that?" Old John banged the receiver onto the hook, and launched what would undoubtedly have been a classic of denunciatory profanity, had it not been interrupted in its inception by Jean, who had slipped into the office unnoticed at the beginning of the telephone conversation.

"Why, Dad!" exclaimed the girl laughing, as the red-faced man whirled upon her in surprise. "What a beastly temper you are in this morning! Who got away, and why are you so anxious to have him caught?"

"Oskar got away," he growled, apparently somewhat mollified by his daughter's tone. "Hicks started for jail with him an' Oskar knocked him down in the alley an' got away."

"Oskar! Jail! What do you mean?"

"I mean just what I say," answered McNabb, meeting the girl's startled gaze squarely. "A thirty thousand dollar sable coat is missing from the store, and no one except Oskar and I had access to the fur safe. He made up a cock-an'-bull story about letting you wear it Saturday to show up Mrs. Orcutt. He claims he went to the theatre to enjoy the effect on Mrs. Orcutt, when he discovered that you were wearing, not the Russian sable that you had worn from the store, but a baum marten coat. He hurried to the store to find that both the sable and the marten coats were gone—"

Old John noticed that as he talked the color receded slowly from the girl's face, leaving it almost chalk white, and then suddenly the color returned with a rush that flamed red to her hair roots. But he was totally unprepared for the sudden fury with which she faced him.

"And you had him arrested! Oskar arrested like a common thief! Are you crazy? You know as well as I do that he never stole a pin—"

"No, he never stole a pin, but there's some little difference in value between a pin and a thirty thousand dollar coat. They say every man's got his price."

"It's a lie!" cried the girl, stamping her foot. "But even if it were true, his price would be so big that there isn't money enough in this world to even tempt him! You ought to be ashamed of yourself! Think what people will say!"

"I don't care what they say. He's got that coat, an' I'm right here to see that he gets just what's comin' to him."

"Well, what people will say won't hurt Oskar!" cried the girl. "They'll all know he didn't steal your coat! They'll say you're a fool! That's what they'll say—and they'll be right, too! It won't take him long to prove his innocence, and then what will people think of you?"

James Hendryx

"He ain't got a show to prove his innocence," retorted McNabb. "Your own testimony will convict him. Didn't ye tell me right here in this room within the hour that the coat ye brought in was the one ye wore from the store, an' the one ye wore to the theatre?"

"And I thought it was," flared the girl. "But if Oskar says it wasn't then it wasn't. And let me tell you this—if you're depending on my testimony to convict him, you might as well have him turned loose right this minute! Because I won't say a word at their old trial. They can put me in jail, too, but they can't make me talk. The whole thing is an outrage, and I'm going right straight down to the jail and tell them to let him out this minute—"

"He's out all right," retorted McNabb. "He knocked Hicks down and escaped on the way to jail."

"I'm glad of it! I hope he broke that nasty old Hicks's head! And if they catch Oskar you had better see that they let him go at once—unless you want to see your own daughter married to a jailbird!"

XII

It was nine o'clock that evening when, growling and grumbling, Hicks himself moved heavily down the short corridor of the jail, and unlocked the door of the cell that held Oskar Hedin. "Come on out!" he commanded.

Hedin stepped in the corridor, and looked inquiringly into the officer's face. "What's up?" he asked.

"Bailed out," growled Hicks.

"Bailed out! Why, who—?"

"I don't know, an' don't give a damn. Someone that's got more money than brains. I wouldn't trust you as far as I could throw a bull by the tail, an' you needn't think I've forgot the poke in the jaw you give me. I'll git you yet."

Hedin paused upon the steps of the police station and glanced across the street where a light burned in the office of Hiram P. Buckner, attorney-at-law. Buckner held the reputation of being by far the most able lawyer in the vicinity, and Hedin's first impulse was to retain him. He crossed the sidewalk and paused abruptly as he remembered that Buckner was McNabb's attorney. Of course, the prosecution of his case would be in the hands of the state, but—why jeopardize his own case by employing a man who stood at the beck and call of the very man who was pushing his prosecution? He turned and proceeded slowly toward his hotel, and as he passed down the street a man stepped from the office of the attorney and followed. He was a large man, muffled to the ears in a fur coat. He followed unnoticed, into the hotel and up the stairs, and when Hedin entered his room and switched on the light the man stepped across the threshold and closed the door behind him. He turned and faced Hedin, throwing back the collar of his coat. Hedin gasped in amazement. The man was old John McNabb, and to his utter bewilderment, Hedin caught a twinkle in the old Scot's eye.

XIII

"'Tis the truth, I'd never ha' know'd ye, an' ye hadn't told me who ye was," welcomed old Dugald Murchison, as he gripped Hedin's hand in the door of the little trading post on the shore of Gods Lake. "Knock the snow from your clothes an' come in to the stove. You're just in time, for by the signs, the storm that's on us will be a three days' nor'easter straight off the Bay. Ye'd of had a nasty camp of it if ye'd of been a day later."

"The guide saw it coming, and we did double time yesterday, and to-day we didn't stop to eat."

Murchison nodded. "Ye come in up the chain of lakes from the south. 'Tis a man's job ye've done—this time o' year. Ye come up from Lac Seul, an' by the guide ye've got, I see the hand of John McNabb in your visit. For old Missinabbee won't go into the woods with everyone, though he'd go through hell itself for John McNabb. But come on in an' get thawed out while the Injun 'tends to the dogs, an' then we'll eat."

"Has Wentworth arrived yet?" asked Hedin, as he followed the factor toward the stove at the rear of the trading room.

Murchison shook his head. "Ye're the first this winter. But

who's Wentworth? An' what'll he be doin' here? An' what are ye doin' here yourself? I suppose it had to do with John's pulp-wood, but the options don't expire till sometime in the summer. Why didn't he come himself?"

It was a long story Hedin unfolded as he and Murchison sat late over their pipes beside the roaring stove in the long, low trading room. The factor puffed in silence without once interrupting until the younger man had finished.

"So John is really goin' to build a paper mill up here? But why did John hire this Wentworth if he figured he couldn't trust him, an' why did he have ye under arrest an' bail ye out? Unless—"

The old factor paused and puffed at his pipe the while his eyes were fixed upon the deep shadows at the far corner.

"Unless what?" asked Hedin eagerly. "I thought, at first, that he believed me guilty of stealing the coat," he went on when Murchison didn't answer. "I know now that he didn't, but when I asked him the reason for my arrest, he only laughed and said that it was all part of the game." Then the younger man's voice dropped, and Murchison noted that the look of eagerness had faded from his face. "As to the hiring of Wentworth," continued Hedin, "that is another matter."

The factor rose slowly and, crossing to the door, opened it and hastily closed it again as a swirl of fine snow-powder enveloped him. Hedin caught the muffled roar of the wind, and in the draught of cold air that swept the room, the big swinging lamp flared smokily. Murchison returned to his chair and filled his pipe. "How's John's daughter comin' along?" he asked between puffs of blue smoke.

"Why, Miss McNabb is very well, I believe," answered

Hedin, a bit awkwardly. "You were right about that storm," Hedin hastened to change the subject. "I'm mighty glad we made Gods Lake to-day, or we would have been held up for the Lord knows how long."

Murchison suppressed a smile, and hunched his chair a bit nearer the stove. "When all's said an' done then, the case stands about like this. This engineer will be along in a few days to begin work locatin' the power dam, an' lookin' up more pulpwood. John believes that Wentworth will let the options expire, an' then swing the stuff over to this man Orcutt an' his crowd—an he's sent you up to block the game."

Hedin nodded. "That's it."

"You're my clerk, an' your name's Sven Larson—that's a good Scandinavian name—an' you don't know nothin' about pulp-wood, nor options. I guess it would be best if we could put him up right here. We could be watchin' him all the while without seemin' to."

"I wonder when Wentworth will be here?" speculated Hedin.

"There's no tellin'. It's accordin' to the outfit he packs an' the guide he's got. They'll have to camp for the storm, an' the snow will slow them up one-half. The storm will last three days or four, an' after that, a day, mebbe a week. Anyways, 'twill give ye time to learn the duties of a factor's clerk, which is a thing the Company has never furnished at Gods Lake, but if John McNabb foots the bill, they'll not worry. 'Twould be better an' ye could play the dolt—not an eediot, or an addlepate—but just a dull fellow, slow of wit, an' knowin' nought except of fur."

Hedin laughed. "That won't bother me in the least."

Murchison shook his head. "'Twill not be so easy as ye think. Askin' foolish questions here an' there, forgettin' to do things ye're told to do, ponderin' deep over simple matters, an' above all ye're to neither laugh nor take offense when I berate ye for a dullard. Ye get the idea—your knowledge of fur is your only excuse for livin'?"

"I get it," smiled Hedin.

Murchison studied the younger man intently. "This Went-worth—how well did ye know him? Or, rather, how well did he know you?"

"You are wondering whether he will recognize me?"

The factor nodded. "Yes, I would not have known ye, for as I remember ye wore a mustache, an' were smooth of chin an' jaw, an' of course, ye wore city clothes. But one who had known ye well wouldn't be so easy fooled."

"He won't recognize me. We have met only·a few times. But even if he had known me much better I wouldn't be afraid, because when I left Terrace City dressed in these togs, and carrying a lumberjacks' turkey on my back, I stopped into a cigar store and inquired the way to the station. The clerk who has seen me every day for years pointed out the way without a flicker of recognition in his eyes—and I didn't have this stubby beard then either."

Murchison seemed satisfied, and after showing his new clerk to his bed, he returned to the stove and knocked the ash from his pipe. "John is canny," he grinned. "As canny in the handlin' of women, as of men. He'll have the son-in-law he wants, an' careful he'll be that he's the man of the lass's own choosin'."

XIV

On the day after the big storm old Missinabbee returned to the southward, and the following day Wentworth arrived at the post, cursing his guide, and the storm, and the snow that lay deep in the forest. The half-breed refused to stop over and rest, but accepted his pay and turned his dogs on the back-trail. And as Murchison accepted McNabb's letter of introduction from Wentworth's hand in the door of the post trading room, his eyes followed the retreating form of the guide. For he had caught a malevolent gleam of hate that flashed from the narrowed black eyes as the man had accepted his pay.

"Ye have not seen the last of yon," he said, turning to Wentworth with a nod of his head toward the breed. "Alex Thumb is counted a bad man in the North. I would not rest so easy, an' he was camped on my trail."

Wentworth scowled. "Worthless devil! Kicked on my bringing my trunk. Wanted me to transfer my stuff into duffle bags and carry a pack to ease up on his dogs; and then to top it off with, he wasn't going to let me ride on the sled. But I showed him who was boss. I hired the outfit and believe me, I rode whenever I felt like it. He may have you fellows up here bluffed, but not me."

"Well, 'tis none of my business. I was only givin' ye a friendly warnin'. Come on now till I get my glasses on, an' we'll see what ye've got here."

Presently he folded and returned the brief note. "An' now what can I do for ye? Will ye be makin' your headquarters here, or will ye have a camp of your own down on the river?"

"I think I'll stay here if there's room. When I'm exploring the river I can take a light outfit along."

"There's plenty of room. There's an empty cabin beside the storehouse, an' I'll have a stove set up, an' your things moved in. Ye'll take your meals with me. There's only a couple of Company Injuns, an' my clerk." Murchison paused. "Sven!" he called. "Sven Larson! Where are ye? Come down out of that fur loft! I've a job for ye."

Slow, heavy footsteps sounded upon the floor above, and a moment later two feet appeared upon the ladder, and very deliberately the clerk negotiated the descent.

"Sven Larson, this is Mr. Wentworth. He's from the States, an' he's goin' to live in the cabin. Take Wawake an' Joe Irish an' set up a stove in there, an' move the stuff in that lays outside."

Hedin acknowledged the introduction with a solemn bob of the head, and as he stared straight into Wentworth's face he blinked owlishly.

"This stove?" he asked, indicating the huge cannon stove in which the fire roared noisily.

"No! No! Ye numbskull! One of them Yukon stoves. An' be

quick about it."

"What stuff?"

"The stuff that lays outside the door—Wentworth's stuff, of course!'

"In the cabin?"

"Yes, in the cabin!" cried the factor impatiently. "Ye didn't think ye was to put it in the stove, did ye?"

Hedin moved slowly away in search of the Company Indians, and Wentworth laughed. "Hasn't got quite all his buttons, has he?" he inquired. "I should say the Company had treated you shabbily in the matter of a clerk."

"Well, I don't know," replied Murchison. "I could have had worse. 'Tis not to be gainsaid that he's slow an' heavy of wit in the matter of most things, but the lad knows fur. More than forty years I've handled fur, an' yet to-day the striplin' knows more about fur, an' the value of fur, than I ever will know. An' then there's the close-mouthedness of him. Ye tell him a thing, an' caution him to say naught about it, an' no bribe nor threat could drag a word of it from his lips. So, ye see, for the job he's got, I could scarce hope for better."

"I presume he knows only raw furs," said Wentworth casually. "He could, of course, have no knowledge of the finished product."

"An' there ye're wrong. Of his early life I know nothing except that he's a foreigner, raised in the fur trade. He can spot topped or pointed furs as far as he can see them, an' as for appraisin' them, he can tell almost to a dollar the value of any piece ye could show him. But—"

The door opened and Murchison turned to greet a newcomer. "Hello, Downey!" he called. "'Tis a long time since ye've favored Gods Lake with a visit. Come up to the stove, lad, an' meet Mr. Wentworth.

"Mr. Wentworth, this is Corporal Downey, of the Royal Northwest Mounted Police." At the word police Wentworth started ever so slightly, but caught himself on the instant. He searched the keen gray eyes of the officer as he extended his hand, but if Downey noticed the momentary trepidation he gave no sign.

"So you're Wentworth," he remarked casually, as he swung the light pack from his shoulders.

"*Captain* Wentworth."

"Oh," Downey accorded him a slanting glance, and entered into conversation with Murchison.

"You knew my name, do you want to see me?" Wentworth interrupted after a wait of several minutes.

"No, not in particular. Only if I was you I'd beware of a dark-haired man, as the fortune-tellers say."

"What do you mean?"

"I met Alex Thumb a piece back on the trail."

"Well, what of it? What has that got to do with me?"

"I don't know. He mentioned your name, that's all. An' I just kind of surmised from the way he done it that you an' him didn't part the best of friends."

"I hired him for a guide, and he undertook to give me my orders on the trail. But I soon showed him where he stood."

Downey nodded. "He's counted bad medicine up here."

"I guess he won't bother me any; I'm here to stay."

"No, he won't be apt to *bother* you any. Probably kill you, though, if you don't keep your eyes open. But don't worry about that, because if he does I'll get him."

"He can't bluff me. I served with the engineers in Russia."

"You'll be servin' with the devils in hell, too, if you don't quit makin' enemies of men like Alex Thumb."

"They didn't use up *all* the brains, when they made the Mounted, Captain."

"*Corporal*'ll do me," corrected the officer. "I wasn't with the engineers—in Russia. I was only in the trenches—in France."

As Downey slung his pack to his shoulders the following morning he stepped close to Murchison. The trading room was deserted save for those two, but the officer lowered his voice. "Wentworth ain't the only one around here that needs watchin'," he said warningly.

"What do ye mean?"

"I mean your clerk ain't the fool he lets on he is. That room you put me in was next to his. The chinkin's fallen out in spots, an' his light was lit late, so I just laid in my bunk an' glued my eye to the crack. He was readin'—an' enjoyin' what he read. He'd lay down the book now an' then an' light a good briar pipe. I'd get a good look into his face then, an' he's no more a fool than you or I. He's damned smart lookin'. An' the books he had laid out on the table wasn't books a fool would be readin'. He was careful to hide 'em away when he rolled in—an' he cleaned his fingernails with a white handled dingus, an' brushed his teeth, an' put the tools back in a black leather case that had silver trimmin's. Believe me, there's somethin' comin' off here between now an' summer, an' I'm goin' to ask for the detail!"

Murchison laughed. "Come on back, Downey, and you'll see the fun. An' I ain't so sure you won't be needed in your official capacity. But don't bother your head over Sven Larson. Remember this: it takes a smart man to play the fool, an' play it right. That's why John McNabb sent him up here. An' his name ain't Larson; it's Hedin. He's John's right-hand man—an' if I mistake not someday he'll be his son-in-law."

"Oh, I'll be back all right," grinned Downey. "I've got a hunch that maybe I'll be needed."

"Ye wouldn't be sorry to have to arrest Wentworth for some kind of thievery, would ye, Downey? I could see ye distrusted him from the moment ye laid eyes on him."

"U-m-m-m," answered Downey. "I was thinkin' more of, maybe, bringin' in Alex Thumb—for murder."

A week later Murchison accompanied Wentworth upon a ten-day trip, during the course of which they visited the proposed mill site, the McNabb holdings, and a great part of the available pulp-wood territory adjoining. With Murchison's help, Wentworth sketched a map of the district that showed with workable accuracy the location of lakes and streams, together with the location of Government and Hudson's Bay Company lands. This done, he secured an

Indian guide and proceeded to lay out and blaze the route of the wagon road to the railway.

By the middle of May the snow had nearly disappeared, and the first of June saw the rivers running free of ice. It was then that Wentworth "borrowed" Sven Larson from the factor and dropped down Gods River in a canoe to its confluence with the Shamattawa. Camp was made at the head of the rapids. Thereafter for five days Hedin worked under Wentworth's direction, while the engineer ran his levels and established his contour. In the evenings as they sat by the campfire smoking, Hedin preserved the same stolid silence that he had studiously observed since the coming of Wentworth.

"Murchison says you know all about fur," Wentworth suggested one evening. "And the finished fur? Do you know that, too—about, well, for instance kolinsky, and nutria, and Russian sable?"

"Kolinsky and nutria are no good. We do not have them here. Russian sable, and sea otter, and black fox, they are the best furs in the world. We do not have them here, either, except once in a while a black, or a silver fox."

"A coat of Russian sable would be very valuable?"

"Yes. Real Russian sable, dark, and well silvered, would be very valuable."

"How much would one be worth?"

"Nobody can tell unless they can see it. It is all in the matching."

For a full minute Wentworth studied the face across the little fire, the face with the unkempt beard, and the far-off, pondering eyes.

"I have a Russian sable coat," ventured Wentworth.

The factor's clerk gazed at him with unwinking blue eyes, and the head wagged slowly. "No. Russian sable is woman's fur. They do not make men's coats of Russian sable."

"But this is a woman's coat," explained Wentworth. "I got it in Russia when I was in the Army. She was a Russian princess and I helped her escape from the country at great risk to myself. It was in the winter, in the dead of night, and a terrible blizzard was raging. When she safely crossed the border she thanked me with tears in her eyes and begged me to take her coat in payment, as she had no money. I refused, but she tossed it into my arms, and disappeared into the night."

"Maybe she died in the storm without her coat."

"Why, no—you see, she had—that is, I had arranged for a car—a sleigh, I mean, to meet her there with plenty of robes. But what I want to get at, is this. If I show you this coat will you promise not to say a word to Murchison about it? I do not want him to know I have it. He would want to buy it, and he is my friend and I do not want to refuse him. But I do not want to sell the coat, because sometime I am going to return it to its original owner. But first I should like you to tell me what it is worth. Can you tell me that? And can you remember never to tell Murchison that I have the coat?"

Hedin nodded. "Yes, I can tell you how much the coat is worth when I see it and feel it. And I will not tell Murchison. That is why I am smart, and others are foolish. Because they tell me what they know, and I listen, and pretty soon I know that, too. But I do not tell what I know, and they cannot listen. So I know what they know, and they do not know what I know, and that is why I am wise and they don't know hardly anything at all."

"Everything coming in, and nothing going out," laughed Wentworth. "That's right, Sven; you've got the system. We will finish here to-morrow, and then we will return to the post, and you can come to my cabin, and I'll show you the fur."

XV

Ever since the evening in camp when Wentworth had confided in him that he had the coat, Hedin had been debating his course of procedure. His first impulse had been to denounce Wentworth to his face, to seize the coat and obtain the engineer's arrest. He knew that Downey expected to return to the post—but there was Jean to consider. Jean—the girl of his fondest dreams, who had forsaken him and fallen under the spell of the courtly manners of the suave soldier-engineer. What would Jean think? If she loved the man she would never believe in his guilt. She would believe, with a woman's irrational loyalty, that he, Hedin, had in some manner contrived to place the coat in Wentworth's possession, and he knew that the engineer would never cease to proclaim that he had been made the dupe of a scheming lover. The case against the man must be plain. When Jean could be shown that Wentworth deliberately endeavored to cheat her father, she would then believe that he stole the coat. She would be saved from throwing herself away, and he—Hedin's lips moved, "I will hire out to the Company, and ask to be sent to the northern-most post they've got."

Upon his arrival at the post, Wentworth made out two reports, one to McNabb and the other to Orcutt, which he dispatched to the railway by a Company Indian. Late in the afternoon, as he was polishing his instruments in the little cabin, the figure of Sven Larson appeared in the doorway. The engineer motioned him to enter and close the door behind him. "Where is Murchison?" he asked, glancing through the window toward the post.

"He has gone in a boat with Wawake to set the fish nets."

Without a word Wentworth stepped across the room, unlocked his trunk, and from its depths drew the sable coat that Hedin had last seen upon the shoulders of Jean McNabb as she walked from the store upon that memorable Saturday. With a conscious effort he controlled himself, and reaching out his hand took the coat and carried it to the window. He was conscious that the engineer's eyes were fastened intently upon him as, inch by inch, he carefully examined the garment whose every skin—every hair, almost—was familiar to him. Still holding the coat, he spoke more to himself than to Wentworth. "A fine piece. All good dark Yakutsk skins. And the matching is good. Only one skin a shade off—"

"What's it worth?" asked Wentworth abruptly. "I don't care a damn about the specifications. They don't mean anything to me. I knew it was a fine garment the minute I spotted it, and I knew Hedin was lying when he said it was a marten."

"Hedin?" queried the clerk. "Was that the name of the princess? She must be a fool to say this is a marten."

"No, no! Hedin is a man. And he is a fool, all right. Fool enough to let a damn fool girl make a fool of him—"

Wentworth suddenly saw a blinding flash of light. He felt himself falling; then he lay very still as a shower of little star-like sparks flowed upward from a black abyss.

The instant he struck, Hedin realized the folly of his act. He would have given all he possessed to have recalled the blow. McNabb had trusted him to carry out a carefully laid plan— and he had failed. He remembered how the old Scot had told him frankly that Jean had fallen in love with Wentworth, and personally, while he believed him to be a good engineer, he wouldn't trust him out of his sight. And then he had outlined the scheme he had laid for showing him up so that Jean would be convinced of his crookedness. And now he had spoiled it all.

The man on the floor stirred restlessly. The thought flashed into Hedin's brain that there might still be a chance. If he played his part well, it was possible.

The next thing Wentworth knew, Sven Larson was bending over him, bathing his face with a large red handkerchief saturated with cold water. "What in hell happened?" muttered the man, as he brushed clumsily at his fast discoloring eye with his hand. With the help of the factor's clerk he sat up. "You hit me! Damn you! What did you hit me for?"

"I am sorry I hit you," answered Hedin heavily. "It is in here —the thing that makes me strike." He rubbed his forehead with his fingers. "It is like many worms crawling inside my head, when one speaks ill of women. My eyes get hot, and the red streaks come, and then I strike. It was such a thing that made me strike Pollak. But I had a hammer in my hand and I looked and saw that Pollak was dead, so I ran away from there and climbed onto the ship. I am glad I did not have a hammer in my hand to-day."

Wentworth regained his feet and glanced at his fast closing eye in the bit of mirror that hung above his wash bench. "So am I," he seconded, forcing a smile. "Where did all this happen? Who was Pollak, and where did the ship take you?"

"It was in London in the place of Levinski, the furrier. Pollak and I worked for him in the sorting of skins. The ship took me to Port Nelson. It was a Hudson's Bay Company ship, and I hired out to the Company and they sent me here to Gods Lake. I like it here."

"So that's it, is it? Well, now you listen to me. We'll just forget the black eye and make a little trade. You keep still about the sable coat, and about hitting me, and I'll keep still about your killing Pollak. Mind you, if I should tell Murchison you had killed a man he would send you back to London, and they would hang you."

"Yes, they would hang me because I killed Pollak. But I do not tell Murchison things that I know. If you do not tell him I killed Pollak, he will not send me back to get hung."

XVI

When John McNabb read Wentworth's report, he reached for his telephone and called Detroit. "That you, Beekman?" he asked, recognizing the voice of the senior partner of one of the foremost engineering firms in the country. "How about you—all set for that Gods Lake job? Just got the preliminary report. Everything O. K. Plenty of water, plenty of head, and we can get it without spreading the reservoir over the whole country. Hustle that road through as fast as you can. Hundred miles of it—only about eight or ten miles of swamp. We can truck the material in quicker than by shipping it clear around through the Bay and track-lining it up the river. Few small bridges, and one motor ferry. Make it good for heavy work. Put on men enough to complete the road in a month at the outside. Most if it will only be clearing out timber and stumps. As soon as the road is done we'll begin to shoot in the cement. Get at it on the jump now, an' I'll see you in a day or two."

The days following the return of Wentworth and Hedin from the survey of the rapids were busy ones at the little post on Gods Lake. For it was the time of the spring trading, and from far and near came the men of the outlands, bringing in their harvest of fur.

The post flag floated gaily at the staff head, and in the broad clearing about its base were pitched the tepees of the fur bringers.

Each rising sun brought additional wilderness gleaners from afar, and additional children, and many additional starving dogs. For these days were the gala days of the Northland; days of high feast and plenty, of boastings, and recountings, and the chanting of weird chants.

The crudity, the primitive savagery of the scene gripped Hedin as nothing had gripped him before. He was astonished that the setting held for him so little of surprise. He fitted into the life naturally and perfectly as though to the manner born. But his own astonishment was as nothing as compared to the astonishment of Murchison, who stood close as Hedin broke open and sorted the packs of fur. Time and again his swift appraisal of a skin won a nod of approval from the factor, who received the skins from his hands and paid for them in tokens of made beaver.

"I do not understand it," said Murchison, between puffs of his pipe, as at the end of a day he and Hedin sat in the doorway of the trading room and watched the yellow flames from a hundred campfires stab the black darkness of the night, and send wavering shadows playing in grotesque patterns upon the walls of the tepees. The harsh din of the encampment all but drowned the factor's words, and Hedin smiled.

"Do not understand what?" he asked.

"'Tis yourself I do not understand. Ye've never handled raw fur, yet in the handling of thirty packs I have not changed the rating of a skin. By your own word, 'tis your first venture into the North, yet since the day of your coming ye have behaved like a man of the North. The Indians distrust a newcomer. They are slow to place confidence in any white man. An' yet, they have accepted your judgment of fur without question. An' a good half of them ye call by name. 'Tis a combination unheard of, an' to be believed only when one sees it."

"And yet it is very simple," explained Hedin. "For years I have studied fur—finished fur—and in the study I have read everything I could find about fur, from the habits of the animals up through their trapping, and the handling of the skins in every step of their preparation. And as for the Indians themselves, I have merely moved about among them and got acquainted, as I would do in a city of white men."

Murchison interrupted him with a snort. "An' a thousand would try it, an' one succeed! 'Tis no explanation ye've given at all. Ye cannot explain it. 'Tis a something ye have that's bred in the bone. Ye're a born man of the North—an' God pity ye for the job ye've got! Cooped up in a store all day with the fanfare of a city dingin' your ears from dawn till midnight, an' beyond! An' what's the good of it? When ye might be living up here in the land that still lays as God made it. The Company can use men like you. You could have a post of your own in a year's time."

For many minutes Hedin puffed at his pipe. "I am glad to hear that," he said at length, "for I am not going back."

"Not going back!" cried Murchison. "D'ye mean it? An' what about that lass of John McNabb's?"

"That lass of John McNabb's has chosen another," answered Hedin in a dull tone.

It was the seventh of June when Wentworth had dispatched the Indian with the reports to McNabb and to Orcutt, and thereafter he settled himself for three weeks of waiting. The activity at the post bored and annoyed him. He complained of the noisy yapping of the night-prowling dogs, cursed the children that ran against his legs in their play, and when necessity compelled him to cross the encampment, he passed among the tepees, obviously avoiding and despising their occupants.

Upon the fifth or sixth day, to rid himself of annoyance, Wentworth essayed a journey to the rapids, and because no one could be spared from the post, he ventured forth alone. When not more than ten miles from the post, he turned his head, as he topped a rock-ribbed ridge for a casual survey of the broad *brule* he had just crossed. The next instant he brought up rigidly erect as his eye caught a swift blur of motion far back on his trail at the opposite edge of the *brule*. He looked again but could make out only an army of blackened stumps. Entering the scrub with a vague sense of uneasiness, he circled among the stunted trees and took up a position under cover of a granite outcropping that gave him a view of his back trail. He had hardly settled himself before a man stepped from behind a stump and struck out rapidly upon his trail. The man was traveling light, apparently studying the ground as he walked. Wentworth glanced about him and noted that the rocky ridge would give the man scant opportunity for trailing him to his position. The figure was coming up the ridge now. As it passed a twisted pine, Wentworth got a good look into his face, and the sight of it sent cold shivers up his spine that prickled uncomfortably at the roots of his hair. For the face was that of Alex Thumb, and at close range Wentworth could see that the black eyes glittered evilly. Icy fingers gripped the engineer's heart. He felt suddenly weak and cold.

Raising a shaking hand to his forehead, Wentworth withdrew it wet and glistening with sweat. His brain conjured fantastic stories of the powers of the Indian tracker, and fearfully he scanned the rocks over which he had come. Suddenly it occurred to him that if the man were still upon his trail, he would have come up with him before this. Evidently the tracker was wasting no time on the broad rocky ridge, but taking it for granted that his quarry would proceed on his way, figured on picking up the trail again in the softer ground of the next valley; in which case he would soon discover his error and circle to correct it. Discarding his pack, the terrified man swiftly descended the ridge and crossed the *brule* at a run. Gaining the shelter of the forest he paused and looked back. The wide clearing was tenantless, and regaining his breath, he resumed his flight, crashing through patches of underbrush, and splashing through streams until, just at dusk, the lights of the Gods Lake campfires came into view.

Completely done up, he staggered into his cabin and, closing the door, fell sprawling upon his bunk, where for an hour he lay while his overtaxed muscles slowly regained their strength. Then he stood up, lighted his candle, and proceeded to remove the record of his mad flight from his scratched skin and torn clothing.

That evening at supper he was surprised to find that Downey had returned to the post. And he wondered if he only fancied that the officer eyed him meaningly.

He said nothing of his experience, but thereafter he was content to remain at the post, never venturing alone beyond the boundaries of the clearing. He became more and more nervous with the passing of the days. One by one, he checked them off, and during the latter days of June he spent hours pacing restlessly up and down, or making the round of the clearing, shunned by Indian dogs and Indian children, and ignored by their elders. And always three questions were uppermost in his mind: Would Orcutt come? Would McNabb come? Would they both come? And finding no answer, he would continue his restless pacing, or raise the imaginary stakes in his game of solitaire to stupendous proportions.

He became more and more irritable as the tension increased. The breaking of a shoe lace called forth a flow of profanity, and when the mainspring of his watch snapped, he hurled the instrument against the log wall in his senseless rage.

XVII

The morning of June 29th brought Cameron, armed with credentials which empowered him to transact any and all business connected with the pulp-wood holdings of the Canadian Wild Lands Company, Ltd. Murchison introduced him to Wentworth, who insisted that the man share his cabin.

"So you are McNabb's man?" queried Cameron with a smile, as he swung his pack to the floor and seated himself upon the edge of a bunk. "Do you know, we rather hoped I would not find you here."

"Why?" asked Wentworth, returning the smile.

"Pulp-wood has gone up since that contract was made. If the stuff were to revert to us we could do much better with it."

"How much better?"

Cameron shot a keen glance at his questioner. "Well, considerably," he answered non-committally.

"A dollar an acre?"

"Two of them."

A brief silence ensued, during which Wentworth was conscious that the eyes of the other were upon him. "Seven dollars an acre," he said. "Pretty high, isn't it, when you consider the inaccessibility to your markets?"

Cameron laughed. "Inaccessibility to markets don't seem to be worrying McNabb any. Bringing his paper mills into the woods seems to have solved that problem. I was talking to the engineer in charge of his road construction day before yesterday—"

"Engineer in charge of road construction!" exclaimed Wentworth. "What road construction—where?"

"Why, north of here. You knew he was building a tote-road, didn't you? I followed the blazed trail clear down to the rapids of the Shamattawa. And he's pushing it, too—got twenty-five or thirty miles of it ready for traffic."

"No—I didn't know he had begun construction," admitted Wentworth. "I knew there was to be a road—laid it out myself. But I did not know that the work had started."

"Well, it has, and we may as well conclude out business."

"But the options do not expire until noon of July first."

"No, but what is to be gained by waiting here until the last minute? He intends to close the deal, so why not get at it? I suppose you were provided with the necessary funds to make the initial payment?"

Wentworth shook his head. "No," he answered. "In fact I have nothing whatever to do with the transaction. I am an engineer sent up here to locate the mill site, lay out the tote-road, and incidentally, to make a survey of additional pulp-wood holdings. I am surprised to hear that McNabb has begun construction of the road."

Cameron stared at the man in astonishment. "What do you mean?" he asked, "that McNabb has added the expense of road construction to the money he put into the options, without making provision for acquiring title to the property? That does not sound like McNabb—what I've heard of him."

"He has until noon of the first," reminded Wentworth.

"Yes, but where is he? He knows the North, and the hundred-an'-one things that can happen to upset a schedule. If I had as much invested in this thing as he has, you may believe I would have been here with plenty of time to spare."

Wentworth nodded. "So would I. But in case he does not show up, what then? The first man that offers seven dollars an acre, and is prepared to make a substantial payment takes the property?"

"Just so. If McNabb, or his representative, is not here on the stroke of twelve, the day after to-morrow, with tender of a cash payment of ten percent. of the purchase price as stipulated in his contract, then he is out of the reckoning altogether. But why do you ask? You speak as though there were some doubt in your mind as to McNabb's appearance?"

"You can never tell," answered Wentworth. "He told me he would be here himself to close the deal at the proper time. If he does not come, it is no affair of mine, except that I should be out of a job. I need the job, so I tipped off his chief rival capitalist as to the date of expiration, and told him that in case for any reason McNabb fell down on the proposition, he had better show up here at the post on the first day of July with a big bunch of coin." He paused and grinned at

Cameron. "I was merely playing safe. If McNabb shows up, well and good. If he don't, well and good again—I still have a job, and you get seven dollars an acre, instead of five."

"But will the other be here?"

Wentworth shrugged. "That is what I have been asking myself for a week. Will McNabb come? Will Orcutt come? Or will they both come? In the latter case I may have let myself in for some unpleasant complications. But I had to take a chance—to avoid taking a chance."

Cameron laughed. "Let us hope for your sake that only one of the parties arrives, and for my sake, that it is the rival, for the additional two dollars an acre will mean an additional million for my company."

XVIII

Along toward the middle of the following afternoon Orcutt appeared at the post, accompanied by two guides and two operatives of a detective agency, who were ostensibly merely members of a party of three, but who in reality were the guardians of a certain thick packet of large bills that reposed in the very bottom of a waterproof rucksack.

Into the trading room he stamped, cursing the black flies and mosquitoes whose combined and persistent attack had left his face and neck red and swollen. Hedin was behind the counter, and without a hint of recognition Orcutt inquired the whereabouts of Wentworth. Upon being informed that he was probably in his cabin, he turned on his heel and stamped from the room.

"This is a hell of a country!" he said in greeting, as Wentworth opened his door to admit him. "The damned flies and mosquitoes just naturally eat a man alive!"

"It isn't so bad when you get used to it," laughed Wentworth, and turned toward the man who had risen from his chair. "Mr. Orcutt, this is Mr. Cameron, representative of the Canadian Wild Lands Company."

"Wild lands is right," grinned Orcutt as he acknowledged the other's greeting. "I never saw so much timber or so many insects in my life. And now," he continued, meeting Cameron's eyes, "I'm a busy man, and the sooner I get out of this God-forsaken country, the better I'll like it. Why can't we go ahead and get the business over with?"

"You forget, Mr. Orcutt, that the McNabb options do not expire until noon to-morrow," Cameron answered.

Orcutt nodded impatiently. "Yes, yes, I suppose we've got to wait. But as far as that goes, I don't think we've got to worry any. I always make it my business to keep an eye on the other fellow, and I know to certainty that John McNabb will not be here. As a matter of fact, he has mistaken the day his options expire. He believes he has until the first of August."

Cameron whistled. "Are you sure?" he asked incredulously. "I don't know him personally, but his reputation for shrewdness—"

"And ninety-nine times out of a hundred he's as shrewd as his reputation calls for," interrupted Orcutt, "but this is the hundredth time! He is so dead sure he is right that I don't suppose he has examined his papers in years. John McNabb makes damned few mistakes—I've been more than twenty years waiting for him to make this one. And now, by God, I've got him! What do you hold the timber at?"

"Seven dollars an acre."

"Make it six, and I'll take it. It ought to be worth something not to have to hunt up a buyer."

"It is," answered Cameron. "But seven dollars is the price. In a month—two months it will be eight."

"About two percent down?"

"Ten."

"Ten percent!" raved Orcutt. "Three hundred and fifty thousand dollars! Do you think a man takes a jaunt into the woods with any such amount of money as that in his possession?"

"I think you did. If not, then as you people say in the States, you are out of luck."

"I'll buy an option on it."

Cameron shook his head. "No, the time has come for a sale. We can't afford to hold timber ourselves, and as to finding purchasers, I know a dozen men who would snap it up at seven dollars."

"All right," growled Orcutt. "Make out your papers and I'll sign 'em. At least, we can get the routine business all finished to-day so all there will be left to do to-morrow noon will be to sign up and pay over the money."

"No harm in that," agreed Cameron. "I shall proceed at once to draw up a contract of sale. Just a question or two will give me all the information I need. In the first place, is the prospective purchaser an individual or a corporation?"

"Corporation. The Eureka Paper Company."

"And their home office?"

"Orcutt, Canada."

"Orcutt? Where is Orcutt?"

Orcutt smiled. "There isn't any—now. But there will be one as soon as we start construction of the mill. The enterprise will be of sufficient magnitude to necessitate a town at the mill site, and the name of that town will be Orcutt."

"Very good. I think that is all I need to know."

"About the subsequent payments—" began Orcutt, but Cameron interrupted him:

"Let us not discuss that now. The better way will be for you to allow me to draw up the contract, and then to-morrow morning we can go over it, clause by clause."

"Good idea," agreed Orcutt. "Come on, Wentworth," and leading the way from the cabin, he spent half an hour strolling about among the tepees viewing their owners, their *lares*, *penates* and offspring as he would have inspected an exhibit at a fair. Tiring of this, he led the way to a fallen log at the edge of the clearing, and produced his cigar case.

"How is everything in Terrace City?" asked Wentworth, as he lighted his cigar.

"Oh, about as usual, I guess. Been so damned busy getting this paper deal in shape for the last two months that I haven't had much time to keep track of things. By the way, you remember Hedin—that clerk in old John McNabb's fur department?"

"Yes, I believe I do."

"Well, old John trusted him to the limit—made a kind of a pet of him—and what does the fellow do but slip up to the store one night and steal a Russian sable coat, worth somewhere around thirty thousand. Then the damned fool, instead of getting out of the country, stayed right on the job. Of course old John missed the coat next day, and the night watchman told of Hedin's visit to the store."

"Did he confess?" asked Wentworth a shade too eagerly.

"Confess nothing! He swears he's innocent. But there's nothing to it. They've got the goods on him—everything but the coat. They can't find that, and they never will. I got the story from Hicks, the police chief. Old John had him arrested and he knocked Hicks down and got away. They caught him again, and Judge Emerson fixed his bail at ten thousand. Someone furnished the bail that same night, and Hedin has skipped out, slick and clean. They sure put one over on McNabb—ten thousand for bail, twenty thousand to divide between them, and McNabb is holding the bag."

"And we'll leave him holding the bag again," grinned Wentworth.

"That's what we will. He's been a hard man to down. I don't mind saying it to you, I've laid for him ever since I've been in Terrace City, and I've never been able to get him. Several times I've thought I had him, but he always managed to wriggle out someway. But now he seems to have let down all of a sudden. Either his luck has deserted him, or he has begun to break."

"You are pretty sure he will not be here to-morrow?"

Orcutt nodded. "Dead sure. You were right about his believing that he has till the first of August on those options. I overheard him telling Bronson on the golf links that he had to be in Canada on August first, and that he would leave about the middle of July."

XIX

After breakfast on the morning of the first of July, Orcutt and Cameron repaired to the cabin where, with the rough pine table littered with maps, they discussed the terms and conditions of the contract of sale. While Wentworth, palpably nervous, paced the clearing; his eyes were upon the trails that led into the forest, and out upon the lake, for a sign of a canoe from the southward.

When at last the pros and cons had all been threshed over, clauses inserted, and clauses struck out, Orcutt drew from his pocket a heavy gold watch, and snapping it open, detached it from its chain and laid it upon the table between them. "Half past eleven," he announced. "I suppose you insist upon waiting until the uttermost minute ticks to its close."

"Yes," answered Cameron. "McNabb's options hold good until twelve o'clock."

"I am anxious to get back," said Orcutt, offering his cigar case, "but I don't want to return without having a look at the mill site. How far is it from here?"

"About forty miles. If you leave here right after noon you will make it before noon to-morrow."

"I'll do it, and return the following day."

The two men smoked with their eyes upon the minute hand that slowly crept toward twelve. Now and then Cameron's glance strayed through the window toward the trading post, as though he half expected to see John McNabb step to its door.

"Twelve o'clock!" announced Orcutt, in a voice that held a ring of triumph. "And I don't mind telling you that, sure as I was that McNabb would not be here, I am breathing easier now than I was two minutes ago."

Leaning forward, Cameron verified the announcement, and dipping the pen in ink, he signed the contract and passed the instrument across to Orcutt, who hastily affixed his signature. Then from the fat bundle upon which his elbow had rested, the banker removed the wrapping and counted out three hundred and fifty thousand dollars in gold certificates of five- and ten-thousand dollar denominations. Cameron recounted, and receipted for the money, and after depositing it in his pocket he extended his hand. "I congratulate you, Mr. Orcutt, upon your purchase, and trust that you have launched upon an enterprise that will prove immensely profitable to yourself and your associates. But for the life of me, I cannot understand McNabb's failure to put in an appearance."

Orcutt's eyes flashed. "Nor can I, except on the theory that he is breaking—losing his grip on affairs. For years we have been business rivals, and for years I have tried to get the upper hand of him, but until this moment I have always failed. It will be a different story from now on," he added vindictively. "Never again will he have the old confidence, the nerve and sureness that has been his chief asset. John McNabb is done. But I'm wasting time. I should right now be on my way to the mill site."

"You will wait for dinner?"

"No. We can eat as we travel," he answered impatiently. "Good-by!" And stepping to the door, he called to Wentworth and the guides and plainclothes-men who waited beside the door.

"Come on! We strike out at once for the mill site. The deal is closed, and we're wasting time. We've got a forty mile hike ahead of us! We'll snatch a lunch later. By the way, Cameron, you may not be here when I return, so I will inform you now that until further notice Mr. Wentworth will be our accredited representative in the field. If anything should come up that needs my attention, take it up with him."

"Just put it on paper, Mr. Orcutt," advised the canny Scot, and with a show of impatience Orcutt scribbled the memorandum.

"Where are we going?" asked Wentworth.

"To the mill site. I want to look it over and return here by the day after to-morrow. All ready?"

The guides swung their packs to their backs and struck into the timber, followed closely by the others of the party.

The following day, Orcutt and Wentworth stood at the head of the rapids and Orcutt listened as the engineer, with the aid of his field notes and maps, explained the construction of the dam, and roughly indicated the contour of the reservoir. "But what's this line—the dotted one, that crosses the river just above us?"

"That is our western property line. It crosses about a mile above here, and we are standing about the same distance above the mill site."

"Do you mean that we own only a mile of timber on the big river above this point?"

"Just about a mile. Our property runs a long way up Gods River, and both sides of the Shamattawa below the dotted line."

Orcutt studied the map for a moment. "Who owns the land above here?" he asked sharply.

"The Hudson's Bay Company on the north side, and the Government on the south."

"Well, what in hell is to prevent someone—McNabb, for instance—from buying up that land and starting operations above us? Even if they didn't put in a dam they could raise the devil with us by driving their stuff through. John McNabb knows every trick of the logging game, and when he finds out what has happened he'll go the limit to buck us."

Wentworth considered. "I guess he could do that, all right. We would have to let his stuff through—"

"I'll fix him!" cried Orcutt. "I'll beat him to it! Where do we do business with the Government and the Hudson's Bay Company?"

"With the Government in Ottawa, and the Company in Winnipeg."

"Hell's bells!" cried Orcutt. "That means we'll be gallivanting all over Canada for the next week or ten days. Well, it can't be helped. I know John McNabb well enough not to leave any loop-hole for him to take advantage of." He called to the guides. "Hey, you Injuns! What's the quickest way to the railroad?"

The guides pointed due north. "Mebbe-so wan hondre mile," announced one.

"But," cried Wentworth, "we're going back by way of the post, aren't we?"

"We're going to hit for the railway the quickest way God will let us!"

"But, I—I left something—that is, I have nothing to travel in but these field clothes, and they're shockingly soiled and tattered."

"Soiled and tattered—hell! What's that got to do with saving years of trouble at the mill? Maybe you ain't as pretty as you'd like to be—but, you've got enough on so they can't arrest you—"

Wentworth felt a decidedly uncomfortable thrill at the word "arrest." He was thinking of a certain Russian sable coat that lay in his trunk at the cabin, and guarded from prying eyes by only a flimsy trunk lock. He thought, also, of Downey—and wondered. He would have given much to have returned to that cabin, but a single glance into Orcutt's face stilled any thought of further objection, and he reluctantly acquiesced.

"We can follow the line of the tote-road," he said. "I blazed it to the railway, and by the way, Cameron said that McNabb had already started construction—had twenty or thirty miles of it completed several days ago."

"Started construction?" cried Orcutt. "Construction of what?"

"The tote-road. He figured it would be quicker and cheaper to haul his material for the mill in from the new railway than to ship by boat around through the Bay to Port Nelson, and then drag it up the river by scow."

"And you mean to say he's started the work? Laid out good money on top of what his options cost him—and forgot to take up the options?"

"That's just what he's done, according to Cameron."

Orcutt burst out laughing. "We'll let him go ahead and build the road," he cried. "Every dollar he puts in will be ninety cents saved for us. It may be two or three weeks before he finds out that he has lost the timber, and possibly the road will be completed by that time. Then I'll buy it in for almost nothing. McNabb has certainly gone fluie! And in the meantime we will use his road to haul in our own material. I'll wire Strang to begin hustling the stuff through."

XX

After watching Orcutt depart, Cameron folded his maps and his papers and walked around to the trading room where Murchison and his clerk were comparing the skins of a silver gray and a black cross fox.

The clerk greeted him with a smile. "Just the man I wanted to see, Mr. Cameron. In fact I was about to go in search of you."

Cameron stared at him in surprise. During the day or two he had spent at the post, he had come to regard the clerk as a stupid, morose individual, whose only excuse for existence, as Murchison had said, was his knowledge of fur. But here was this unkempt clerk actually smiling, and addressing him as a man of affairs. He glanced inquiringly at Murchison before replying. "And why should you go in search of me?"

"As accredited representative of the Canadian Wild Lands Company, I have business to transact with you." Hedin stepped forward and extended a paper. "I represent John McNabb."

"John McNabb!" cried Cameron, staring at him as though he had taken leave of his senses. "You mean—"

Hedin interrupted him, speaking crisply. "I mean that this paper, as you will note, is a power of attorney which gives me authority to transact any and all business for Mr. McNabb, concerning the purchase of certain pulp-wood lands."

"Dut, man!" cried Cameron excitedly.

Ignoring the interruption, Hedin continued. "And I hereby, in the presence of Mr. Murchison, tender payment of ten percent, of the purchase price, as provided in the terms of the option contract."

"But you're too late!" roared Cameron. "McNabb's options expired at noon! The land has been sold and payment accepted! Good Lord, man! Do you mean that McNabb sent you up here to close the deal, and you deliberately neglected to attend to it until the options had expired?"

"Too late?" smiled Hedin. "What do you mean, too late? The options do not expire until noon," he paused and glanced up at the clock that ticked upon the wall, "and it still lacks twenty-five minutes of twelve."

Cameron stared at the clock. "It is a trick!" he cried. "You turned the clock back! What time have you, Murchison?"

The factor meticulously consulted his watch. "Twenty-four minutes to twelve," he announced.

"You are into it, too!"

Murchison smiled. "Look at your own watch," he suggested. "What time have you got?"

Cameron drew out his timepiece and stared at it blankly. "He laid his watch on the table between us," he said in a bewildered tone, "and not until the hands reached twelve were the papers signed and the money paid."

"What do you mean?" asked Hedin. "The papers signed, and the money paid?"

"Why Orcutt, president of the Eureka Paper Company, bought the land after McNabb's options expired. Wentworth is his representative."

"But McNabb's options have not expired," insisted Hedin. "His payment has been tendered in the presence of a witness before the time of their expiration. Any sale or contract entered into with Orcutt or anyone else concerning title to these lands is, of course, void."

Cameron continued to stare at his watch. "I do not understand it," he muttered.

"I think I do," offered Hedin. "Was it Orcutt's watch you consulted?"

"Yes, he laid it on the table, and we watched the hands mark off the time."

"And you were an hour fast! Orcutt carried Terrace City time, which is an hour faster than standard. It is the so called daylight saving plan adopted by many cities and villages in the United States by act of council. All that, of course, has no bearing on McNabb's options, so there is nothing for you to do but accept payment and return Orcutt his money."

"But you were here all the time!" cried Cameron. "And you must have known what was going on. Why didn't you make yourself known? Why did you let me go ahead with Orcutt?

We could have had the business over and done with two days ago—and no complications."

Hedin laughed. "You will have to take that up with Mr. McNabb. I was following out instructions to the letter. And those instructions were very specific about not closing the deal within half an hour of the expiration of the options."

"But what was his idea?"

"As I said before, you will have to ask him. He had a reason, you may be sure. I have noticed in my association with John McNabb that there is generally a reason for the things that he does—though in many instances the reason is beyond me."

Cameron's exasperation at the sudden turn of events subsided. He even managed a smile. "He was within his rights," he admitted, "and as you say, he must have had a reason. But I don't understand it. Wentworth was McNabb's man too—until he swung over to Orcutt. Yet he never suspected you were anything but Murchison's clerk."

Hedin laughed. "The reputation of being a fool doesn't hurt anyone. It is rather an advantage at times."

"You have played your part well," admitted Cameron. "And McNabb has played his part well—whatever that part is. Orcutt said he was losing his grip, was in his dotage. Well, he will not be the first man that has had to change his mind. He has gone to inspect the mill site and will return day after to-morrow. Wentworth accompanied him. I imagine we will have an interesting half-hour when they find out that the deal is off."

The formalities of payment were soon over with, and the moment they were completed, Hedin despatched a messenger with a telegram to his employer.

When John McNabb received the message he grinned broadly, and for several minutes sat at his desk and stabbed at his blotter with his pencil point. "So, Orcutt, Wentworth & Company set out to down poor old John McNabb," he muttered. "I kind of figured rope was all Wentworth wanted to hang himself with—an' rope's cheap. But Orcutt an' his Eureka Paper Company—now he must have gone to quite a little bother, first an' last, an' some expense. Too bad! But I won't worry about that—he ought to 'tend to his bankin'. Guess I'll be startin' North in about ten days."

A week later McNabb got another wire from the engineer in charge of his road construction. As he read and reread it, a slow smile trembled upon his lips and widened into a broad grin.

"Sixty-five miles of road completed. Eureka Paper Company cement and material piling up at road head. Have their own trucks. Shall we let them use road?"

The grin became an audible chuckle. "I don't understand it. Orcutt must have cleared out so quick he don't know the deal is off." Then he called a messenger and sent two telegrams. The first in answer to the one just received.

"Double your force and hurry road to completion in shortest possible time. Allow all Eureka Paper Company goods to be delivered as fast as received. Facilitate delivery same to mill site in every way possible."

The other telegram was to the home office of the engineering firm and read:

"Hold off on purchase of material for mill until further

notice. Writing full particulars."

Then he closed his desk and went home where, a few minutes later, his daughter found him packing his outfit in a well worn duffle bag.

XXI

Ever since Jean's outburst of passion upon the day of Hedin's arrest, a certain constraint had settled upon father and daughter that amounted, at times, to an actual coldness. Neither had mentioned the name of Hedin in the other's hearing, but each evening at dinner, which was the only meal at which they met, the studied silence with which the girl devoted herself to her food bespoke plainer than words that the thought of him was never out of her head.

So it was with some measure of surprise that Old John looked up from his packing at the girl's question: "Where are you going, Dad?"

"North, into Canada. I've business there that needs my attention."

"Will you take me with you?"

"Take ye with me!" he cried in astonishment. "An' what would ye be doin' in the wild country, with the black flies an' mosquitoes in the height of their glory. They'd eat ye alive! An' the trailin'—why, ye've never been outside a town in ye're life!"

"And that is just why I want to go outside one!" answered the girl. "Please, Dad, take me with you. I can keep up on the trail, really I can. Don't I play golf, and tennis, and paddle a canoe, and do everything that anyone can do to keep themselves in shape? I bet right now I can walk as far as you can in the woods or out of the woods. And as for flies and mosquitoes, they won't eat me any worse than they will you, and if worse comes to worst, I can plaster myself with that smelly old dope you carry in that bottle—but I'd almost rather be eaten."

Old John grinned. "Well, I don't know. Maybe the trip would do ye good. An' when ye get there ye may not find it so dull. Wentworth is there an' he'll prob'ly show ye around."

"I don't need Captain Wentworth to show me around," she replied, and McNabb was not slow to note her tone. "Of all people I ever met, I think he's the biggest bore! I don't see what you hired him for."

Old John stared at her in amazement. "Why, it was on your own recommendation—that, an' the fact that I found out he done some really good work on the Nettle River project. But you asked me in so many words to give him a job!"

"Well, if I did, I was an idiot," she replied. "And I guess you'll wish you never hired him. You'll find you've made a grand mess of things!" A high-pitched, nervous quality had crept into the girl's voice, and McNabb saw that she was very near to tears. "Do you know what they're saying?" she cried. "They're saying that Oskar has jumped ten-thousand-dollar bail that some friend put up for him! They're liars, and I hate them! Wherever he is, he'll come back at the proper time. He'll show them—and he'll show you, too!" With an effort, the girl steadied her trembling voice. "And when he does come back, he'll find he's got one friend—and I'll—I'll make up for the rest. I'm going to get ready now. I want to get away from it all. When do we start?"

"To-night," answered old John, "on the late train." And when the door closed behind his daughter, he grinned and winked at himself in the mirror.

When old John McNabb and his daughter stepped off the sagging combination coach at the siding which was the northern end of the new tote-road, the first man they saw was Orcutt, resplendent in striped mackinaw, Stetson hat, and high-laced boots. As the banker came toward them, McNabb stared about him in evident perplexity, his glance shifting from the piles of tarpaulin-covered material, to the loaded trucks that with a clash and grind of gears were just pulling out upon the new tote-road that stretched away between the tall balsam spires to the southward.

"Hello, John," Orcutt greeted, lifting his Stetson in acknowledgment of the presence of Jean. "Well, what do you think of it?"

McNabb continued to stare about him. "I don't seem to quite get the straight of it," he said slowly. "Eureka Paper Company," he read the legend emblazoned upon the trucks and tarpaulins scattered all over the foreground. "What does it mean, Orcutt? An' what in the devil are you doin' here? An' what business have those trucks got on my tote-road?"

Orcutt laughed, a nasty, gloating laugh, as he rubbed his hands together after the manner of one performing an ablution. "It means, John," he answered, in a voice of oily softness, "that at last I have caught you napping. The Eureka Paper Company is my company, and the pulp-wood that you held options on is my pulp-wood. I've been waiting a long time for this day—more than twenty years. It's only fair to give the devil his due, John—you've been shrewd. Time and again I almost had you, but you always managed somehow to elude me. There have been times when I could have murdered you, gladly. It wouldn't have been so bad if you had gloated openly when you put one over on me, but your devilish way of apparently ignoring the fact—of acting as though outwitting me were too trifling an occurrence to even notice, at times has nearly driven me crazy—that, and that damned secret laughter I see in your eyes when we meet. Oh, I've waited a long time for my day—but now my day has come! And to think how nearly I missed it! I go back in an hour on the same train that brought you in."

McNabb had listened in silence to the tirade. "But I—I don't understand it. My options—"

"Your options," interrupted Orcutt, and his voice rasped harsh, "expired at noon on the first day of July. At one minute past twelve on that day, the property passed into the hands of the Eureka Paper Company of which I am president. I signed the contract and paid over the money myself at Gods Lake Post."

"Was it July?" mumbled McNabb, apparently dazed. "But— there was Wentworth. He had the papers. Surely he must have known."

Orcutt laughed. "Yes. Wentworth knew. He knew the day you hired him. And he knew that you thought you had until the first of August. It was Wentworth that tipped the deal off to me."

"But—why should he have double-crossed me?"

"Mere matter of business," replied Orcutt. "Figure it out for yourself. If he stayed with you the best he could expect would be a fair salary. With us he was in position to dictate his own terms. They were stiff terms, too, for Wentworth is shrewd. But he has been worth all he cost. He is now secretary of the Eureka, and a very considerable stockholder."

McNabb was silent for what seemed a long time. When at length he spoke, it was in a voice that sounded dull and tired. "But, Orcutt, the tote-road is mine. I built it. It cost me a hundred thousand dollars—that road did. If you hold the property the road is no good to me, and it is valuable to you. Will you buy it?"

"Sure, I'll buy it. I'll buy it for just what I figure it is worth to me. It cost you a thousand dollars a mile. It's worth a hundred to me. Ten thousand dollars is my limit. Take it or leave it. Ten cents on the dollar, John; you may as well save what you can out of the wreck."

"Is that the best you can do by me? Man, it's robbery! I can't afford to lose ninety thousand. It'll cripple me. An' I stood to make a million!"

"Cripple you, eh? Well, it won't hurt my feelings to see you limping. That's the very best we can do. You better take it, and go back to selling your thread. You're getting too old for real business, John—you're done!"

McNabb nodded slowly. "Aye, maybe ye're right, maybe ye're right." The voice sounded old, tired. "I'll let ye know in a few days, Orcutt. Now that I'm up here I think I'll slip down for a visit with my old friend Murchison. He's the factor at Gods Lake. We were boys together, an' together we worked for the Company. He's a friend a man can trust. An' I feel the need of a friend. Ye'll not begrudge us a ride down on one of ye're trucks, will ye, Orcutt?"

Before Orcutt could reply Jean, who had been a silent listener to all that had passed, leaped forward and faced Orcutt with blazing eyes. "You sneak!" she cried. "And all the time I thought you and Mrs. Orcutt were my friends! And all the time you were lying in wait to ruin an old man! You couldn't fight him in the open! You were afraid! But my father is used to fighting men—not cowardly thieves! And as for riding in one of your trucks, I would die first!" She turned to McNabb. "Come on, Dad, we'll walk!"

"But, daughter, it's a hundred miles!"

"I don't care if it is five hundred miles! I'll walk, or crawl if I have to, rather than accept anything from that—that rattlesnake! See, there is a little store. We can lay in some provisions for the trip and it will be loads of fun. It will remind you of your old days in the North."

The girl took his arm, and the two turned abruptly away, leaving Orcutt standing in his tracks watching their departure with somewhat of a grin.

As they came out of the store with bulging pack sacks, they saw him step into the stuffy coach, and a moment later they watched the wheezy little engine puff importantly down the track. Then, side by side they stepped onto the tote-road and were swallowed up between the two walls of towering balsams and spruces.

A mile farther on, a Eureka truck passed them, and the girl, scorning the driver's offer of a lift, brushed its dust from her clothing as though it were the touch of some loathsome thing.

That night they camped on a little hardwood knoll beside a stream, well back from the road. Old John seemed to have regained his usual spirits, and to her utter astonishment the girl surprised a grin upon his face as he put up the shelter. He built a fire, and producing hook and line from his pocket, jerked half a dozen trout from the water, which were soon sizzling in the pan from which rose the odor of frying bacon.

"Do you know, Dad," began the girl, after the dishes had been washed and the man had thrown an armful of green bracken upon the fire to smudge away the mosquitoes. "Do you know I think you are simply wonderful?" She was leaning against his knee, and her eyes looked into his.

"Tush, girl, what ails ye?" said the man, removing his pipe to send a cloud of blue smoke to mingle with the gray of the smudge.

"I mean it, Daddy, dear. You are just wonderful. Oh, I know how disappointed you are. I know just how it hurts to have a man like Orcutt get the best of you. I saw it in your face."

"Did Orcutt see it, d'ye think?"

"Of course he did—and he just gloated."

"U-m-m," said McNabb, and his lips twitched at the corners.

"And on top of all that you can smile!"

"Yup, isn't it funny? I can even grin."

"But, Dad, will it—ruin you? Not that I care a bit, about the money. We can be just as happy, maybe happier, without it. I'm not the little fool you think I am. I have always spent a lot of money because I had it to spend, but if we didn't have it, I could be just as happy making what little I did have go as far as it could. Maybe we'll have to come up here and live in a cabin. I love the North already, and I've hardly seen it. We could have a cabin in the woods, and get some furniture when we could afford it, and then we could arrange it so cozily. Really, I would be crazy about it. And we could have trout every day, and wild ducks, and venison. If we could afford a screened porch we could eat and sleep on it, and in the living room we could have a table—"

"Good Lord, girl, arrangin' furniture again!" cried old John. "An I'd come home some night an' break my neck before I could find the matchbox. If we was to live in a cabin I'd spike the stuff to the floor! But—maybe it won't be so bad as all that."

"I've been hateful to you of late, Dad, because of—of Oskar. But really, you made an awful mistake. I should think you would know that he couldn't have taken that coat. It isn't in him!"

"I never said he ate it," grinned the man.

"Oh, don't joke about it! Dad, I love Oskar. He's—oh, he's everything a man should be, and it hurts me so to have them saying he is a thief. He isn't a thief! And the time will come when he will prove it. Promise me, Dad, that when he does prove it, you will make every effort in your power to right the wrong you have done him."

Old John's hand rested for a moment upon the girl's head. "I promise all that, girl. Surely ye know I can be just. If it is as ye say, I'll more than make it up to him. I promise ye, his name shall not suffer."

"I love you, Dad. I know you are just—but you're a hard-hearted old Scot, just the same. You don't make many mistakes, but you have made two—about Oskar, and about hiring that Wentworth. I told you you'd be sorry."

"Well, maybe ye're right," and John McNabb never blinked an eye.

"See, didn't I just say you were hard-headed? You won't admit you made a mistake even after what Orcutt told you to-day. But tell me honestly, Dad, are you ruined?"

"Well, we won't worry about that, lass. D'ye hear the hoot-owl? I like to hear them of nights. I found one's nest once an' I took the three eggs out an' slipped them under a hen that Mother McFarlane had settin'. It was at Long Lake post, Mother McFarlane was the factor's wife, an' I was his clerk. The eggs had been sat on a long time an' they hatched out before the hen eggs. Ye should have seen Mother McFarlane's face when she caught sight of them chickens! It was one of the best jokes I ever made."

"And here you ought to be as solemn as an owl yourself, and you are talking of jokes. I don't understand you at all."

"Maybe I should be an owl. D'ye notice in the stories, they make the Scots say, 'hoot'? But about Wentworth, now. If we should meet up with him, don't let on ye know anything about my deal with Orcutt. Treat him nice an' pleasant—"

"After what he has done to you?" cried the girl, her eyes flashing.

"Just so. Be nice an' friendly to him—d'ye know what a poker face is?"

"Why, of course! Everybody plays poker in Terrace City."

"Mind ye, ye're settin' in a big game right now—"

"You mean," cried the girl, "that there's a chance? A chance to beat Orcutt yet? Oh, if you only could!"

"Well, we're still settin' in the game—me an' you, daughter. An' let's don't neither one of us throw down our hand till after the draw."

XXII

Toward evening of the fourth day after leaving the railway, the two stepped into the broad clearing that surrounded the Gods Lake post.

"Oh, real Indians!" cried Jean, as she caught sight of the dozen or more tepees that were pitched between the lake and the low log trading post.

"Aye, real Injuns, lass—an' good it is to see them again. It will be the remnant of the spring tradin'. 'Tis about over now, but always there's some of the Injuns will hang around the post all summer."

"They're cooking over open fires, and look, there comes one from the lake with some fish! Oh, don't you just love it?"

They were crossing the clearing, and old John glanced at his daughter with approval. "Aye, I love it. An' proud I am that you love it, too. Ye've taken to the North like a duck takes to water. Ye've trailed like a real sourdough, an' never a word of the hard work an' the discomfort. 'Tis born in ye, lass—the love of the bush—an' I'm glad. I've come to know ye better the last four days than I have in twenty-one years of school, an' dancing an' all the flibberty-jibbitin' nonsense ye carry on."

They had reached the door of the trading room, and the man interrupted her laughing reply. "Wait ye here a minute while I see if Dugald is inside."

Oskar Hedin paused in the act of putting the finishing touches on the edge of his belt ax, and as John McNabb entered the room, he rose hastily to meet him.

"Where's Murchison?" asked the newcomer, and Hedin noted that no slightest hint of recognition flickered in his employer's eyes.

Repressing the desire to laugh, he answered in the slow, dull-witted manner of Sven Larsen. "He is in there," pointing to the door of the factor's room.

"Tell him to come out here," commanded McNabb brusquely.

"Do you want to see him?"

"What in the devil d'ye think I'm waitin' here for? Hurry, now, an' don't be standin' there gawpin'."

Hedin grinned broadly as he entered Murchison's door, and a moment later McNabb's hands were gripped by the two hands of the factor. "It's glad I am to see ye, John. An' how does it feel to get home once more?"

"Ye'll be knowin' yourself how it feels to a man that's been thirty years out of the bush. But where's Hedin?"

"He'll be here directly," answered Murchison. "John, I want ye to meet my clerk, Sven Larsen. He's the best clerk I ever had."

McNabb glanced into the bearded face that blinked stupidly at him. "Ye haven't be'n over favored with clerks, I'd say, Dugald. But how are ye fixed for quarters?"

Murchison laughed. "I guess we can rig up a bunk for ye, John."

"It ain't myself I was thinkin' about. It's the lass. She's had four pretty hard days on the trail, an' she'd be the better for a comfortable bunk."

"The lass!" exclaimed Murchison.

"Jean! Here!" Strong fingers gripped McNabb's arm, and he stared in astonishment into the face of Sven Larsen. The loose-lipped, vapid expression was gone, and the blue-gray eyes stared into his own with burning intensity.

"You don't mean—? Why, Oskar lad!"

"Sh—sh. But she mustn't know! Promise me—both of you! She will be going to bed early, and after supper I'll see you at the landing."

McNabb studied the face quizzically. "Ye fooled me, all right, but I'm doubtin' ye can fool Jean."

"At least, I can try," answered the clerk. "I'll see you at supper," and without waiting for a reply, he ascended the ladder that led to the fur loft.

"Where is the lass? Fetch her in, John." Murchison's eyes twinkled as he stepped closer. "He thinks he's lost her," he whispered. "But tell me, John, d'ye think the lass cares for this damned Wentworth?"

"Who can say?" grinned McNabb. "'Twill not be long now till we can see for ourselves," and stepping to the door he called Jean, who was trying to make friends with a group of Indian children.

"She'll have my room," said Murchison, as he followed McNabb to the door. "An' no bunk, either, but a brass bed that I bought in Winnipeg out of respect for my old bones an' the weakening flesh that covers 'em. You an' me will pitch a tent, an' 'twill be the first time in many years, John, we've slept under canvas together."

The next moment he was welcoming the girl with a deference he would have scarce accorded to royalty.

XXIII

Supper over, McNabb left Jean to be entertained by Murchison, and strolled down to the landing to join Hedin. "Well, how's everything comin'?" he asked, as he seated himself beside the clerk upon a damaged York boat.

"I wired you that the deal was closed, and the pulp-wood is safe. But there have been complications that you could never suspect."

"So?"

"Yes. In the first, you were dead right about Wentworth—about not trusting him. And you knew who he expected to let in on the deal?"

"Why, Orcutt, of course," replied McNabb. "I know all about that. That's why I told ye to hold off till the last minute about closing."

"But you couldn't have foreseen that Orcutt wouldn't bother to set his watch back, or that they would use his watch in concluding their deal."

McNabb shook his head. "No, an' I don't know yet what ye're talkin' about. All I know is, that Orcutt thinks he has got title to the pulp-wood. We met him back at the railway, an' he took pains to tell me about it. What puzzles me is, how did ye work it so that after two weeks have gone by he still thinks he owns the timber?"

"I didn't work it. He came up here on the twenty-ninth and waited around until the first of July. Then he and Cameron went over to the shack and concluded the deal, using Orcutt's watch, which was Terrace City time—an hour fast. Then Orcutt and Wentworth hit straight for the mill site, saying they were coming back in two days. Half an hour later I called Cameron's attention to the error in time and took up the options for you. After the papers were signed he decided to wait for the return of Orcutt and Wentworth. But they didn't return. He waited for a week, and then went to look for them. They haven't shown up yet."

Old John was chuckling aloud. "An' the Eureka Paper Company's stuff is rollin' down my tote-road as fast as they can unload it."

"Do you mean they've started to haul the material for their mill?"

"Aye, not only material but machinery."

"But what's become of Cameron?"

"Losh, lad, I don't even know the man. We won't worry about him."

"But why did you want to put off the closing till the last minute?"

McNabb grinned. "Why did you let Jean wear the sable coat?" he asked in return. "'Twas only to string Orcutt along, thinkin' he had me bested till the last minute—then bring him up with a jolt. I didn't know it would work out so lucky for me."

"How do you mean—lucky?"

"You wait an' see," grinned McNabb. "D'ye know, Orcutt offered me ten thousand dollars for my tote-road? An' it cost me a hundred thousand!"

A long silence followed McNabb's words, during which Hedin cleared his throat several times. The older man smoked his pipe, and cast covert glances out of the tail of his eye. Finally he spoke. "What's on ye're mind, lad? Speak out."

Hedin hesitated a moment and plunged into the thing he had dreaded to say. "Mr. McNabb, I've been up here several months now—" he hesitated, and as the other made no comment, proceeded. "I have come to like the country. It—I don't think—that is, I don't want to go back to Terrace City. You can understand, can't you? You have lived in the North. I wasn't born to be a clerk. I hate it! My father was a real man. He lived, and he died like a man. This is a man's country. I am going to stay." Hedin had expected an outburst of temper, and had steeled himself to withstand it. Instead, Old John McNabb nodded slowly as he continued to puff at his pipe.

"So ye're tired of workin' for me. Ye want to quit—"

"It isn't that. I would rather work for you than any man I ever knew. You have been like a father to me. You will never know how I have appreciated that. I know it seems ungrateful. But the North has got me. I never again could do your work justice. My heart wouldn't be in my work. It would be here."

"An' will ye keep on workin' for Murchison? What will he pay ye?"

"It isn't the pay. I don't care about that. I have no one but myself to think of. And Murchison said that with my knowledge of fur the Company would soon give me a post of my own."

"But—what of the future, lad?"

Hedin shrugged. "All I ask of the future," he answered, and McNabb noted just a touch of bitterness in the tone, "is that I may live it in the North."

"H-m-m," said McNabb, knocking the ashes from his pipe, "I guess the North has got ye, lad. An' I'm afraid it's got Jean. The lass has been rantin' about it ever since we left the railway. But—who is that? Yonder, just goin' into the post? My old eyes ain't so good in the twilight."

"Wentworth!" exclaimed Hedin, leaping to his feet. "Come on! The time has come for a showdown!"

Hedin's voice rasped harsh, and McNabb noticed that the younger man's fists were clenched as he laid a restraining hand upon his arm. "Take it easy lad," he said. "Maybe it's better we should play a waitin' game."

"Waiting game!" cried Hedin. "I've been playing a waiting game for months—and I'm through. Good God, man! Do you think my nerves are of iron? I love Jean—love her as it is possible for a man to love one woman. I have loved her for years, and I will always love her. And I've lost her. That damned cad with his airs and his graces has won her completely away. But, by God, he'll never have her! I'll show him up in his true colors—"

"An' with him out of the way, lad, ye'll then—"

"With him out of the way she'll despise me!" interrupted Hedin. "She will never marry him out of loyalty to you, when she finds out he has tried to knife you. I haven't told you all I know—when he falls, he'll fall hard! But I know what women think, and I know she'll despise me for disguising myself and spying on him."

"If ye know what women think, lad, ye're the wisest man God has yet made, an' as such I'm proud to know ye."

"It is no time to joke," answered Hedin bitterly. "That's a thing I've never been able to fathom, why you always joke in the face of a serious situation, and then turn around and raise hell over some trivial matter that don't amount to a hill of beans."

McNabb grinned. "Do I?" he asked. "Well, maybe ye're right. But listen, lad, I know ye've regard for me, an' I'm askin' as a personal favor that ye hold off a bit with your denouncement of yon Wentworth. Just play the game as ye've been playin' it. Keep on bein' Sven Larsen, the factor's clerk, heavy of wit, an' able with fool questions. Ye've a fine faculty for actin'; for all durin' supper the lass never suspected ye. Keep it up for a while; it won't be for long."

"But what's the good of it? We know as much as we'll ever know. Man, do you know what you're asking? Loving Jean as I love her, I must stand about and play the fool, while that damned thief basks in her favor under my very eyes! If there were a good reason, it would be different. But Wentworth and Orcutt can go no farther; they're done—"

"Aye, but they're not done," interrupted McNabb. "Ye'll be knowin' me well enough to know I always have a reason for the things that I do. It's a hard thing I'm askin' of ye, an' in this case I'll show ye the reason, though 'tis not my habit. D'ye mind I told ye that the Eureka material was rollin' down the tote-road by the truck load? Thousands of dollars worth of it every day is bein' delivered at the mill site. Why? Because for some reason Orcutt has not yet found out that he does not own the timber. The minute he does find out, not another pound will be delivered."

"You mean—?"

"I mean that portland cement, an' the reinforcin' steel, an' plate an' whatever else goes into the construction of a paper mill is bein' set down on the Shamattawa, one hundred miles from a railway at Orcutt's expense. And that every ton of it is stuff that won't pay its way out of the woods. The freight an' the haulin' one way doubles the cost. An' even if he tried to take it out, he'd have a hundred miles of tote-road to build. Eureka freight travels only one way on McNabb's tote-road—an' that way is in!"

Hedin stared at the man in astonishment. "And you can buy it at your own figure!" he cried. "Why, you can prevent even his empty trucks from going back. God, man, it will ruin Orcutt!"

"'Tis his own doin's," answered the man. "'Twill serve him right. He should have 'tended to his bankin' instead of pickin' on poor old John McNabb, that should be back of his counter sellin' thread, as he told me himself. Ten cents on the dollar he offered for my tote-road."

"I'll do it!" exclaimed Hedin. "It will be hard, but it will be worth it, to see that crook get what's coming to him. And then I'm going away. Murchison will give me a letter, and I'll strike the Company for a job."

McNabb nodded. "I guess ye're right, about not goin' back to the store," he said slowly. "Your heart is in the North."

There was a strange lump in Hedin's throat. He glanced into the face of his employer, and was surprised at a certain softness in the shrewd gray eyes that gazed far out over the lake. After a time the old man spoke, more to himself than to him. "Ye could both run down for a month or two in the winter!"

"What?" asked Hedin, regarding the speaker with a puzzled expression. "Both of who? A factor only gets away in the summer."

"So they do—so they do," answered McNabb, absently. "Well, we'll be goin' back now. My engineer, maybe, will be wantin' a conference."

XXIV

A rather strained silence greeted the entrance of McNabb into the trading room. Jean and Murchison occupied the only two chairs the room boasted, and Wentworth leaned against the counter, a half-sneering smile on his lips. McNabb advanced to the group beneath the huge swinging lamp, and Sven Larsen lingered in the shadows near the door. The half-sneer changed to a look of open defiance, as Wentworth faced McNabb. "It seems," he said truculently, "that I am guilty of a serious *faux pas* in mentioning a bit of Terrace City scandal that reached my ears concerning the elopement of your estimable fur clerk, Hedin, and a Russian sable coat. The idiot didn't have the brains to get away with it. If you'd have been wiser you would have waited until you could have laid hands on the coat, and then locked up your fur clerk."

"H-m-m, maybe ye're right," answered McNabb.

"And," continued Wentworth, emboldened by the placidity of the other's tone, "if you had been wiser, you wouldn't have lost your pulp-wood holdings. Oh, there's no use beating about the bush—I knew the minute Jean told me you had come in by the tote-road, that you had seen the Eureka trucks hauling in Eureka material. We put one over on you, McNabb, and you might as well be a sport and make the best of it."

The old Scot nodded thoughtfully. "Maybe ye're right," he admitted. "But wasn't it a bit scurvy trick ye played me, acceptin' my money an' usin' it to double-cross me?"

"Business, my dear man! Merely business! I saw my chance, and I took it, that's all. Ten thousand a year, and a ten percent interest in a paper mill isn't so poor—and I'm not yet thirty. It takes brains to make money, and you can bet I'll make my money before my brain begins to slip cogs. It's expensive—this slipping of cogs."

"Maybe ye're right," repeated McNabb.

"I'll tell the world I'm right! It won't be but a few years till I'll be the big noise around this part of Canada! Brains to figure out a proposition, and nerve to carry it through—that's all it takes to make this old world pay up what it owes you."

"How he hates himself!" exclaimed Jean, and from his position in the shadows, Hedin saw that her eyes flashed.

His heart gave a great bound, and it was with an effort that he restrained himself from pushing into the group. Was it possible—? A step sounded outside, and the next moment the screen door swung open to admit the figure of a man who strode into the lamp-light and glanced about the faces of the assembly.

The man was Cameron.

"A fine two days' stay you made of your trip to the mill site," he grumbled, addressing Wentworth. "I waited here for a week for you or Orcutt to show up, and then I decided to hunt you. I followed you to Winnipeg, and from there to Ottawa, and back again to the head of the tote-road. Orcutt had left for the States the day before I got there, but they said you were down at the mill site. I rode down on a truck only to find that you had come over here for your outfit."

"Well, now you've found me, what's on your mind?" grinned Wentworth.

"I have a memorandum here in my pocket signed by Orcutt in which he authorized you to transact any and all business regarding the pulp-wood lands."

"That's correct," admitted Wentworth. "I am a stockholder, an officer in the company, and its sole representative in the field. Fire away. What's this business that's so all-fired important as to send you chasing all over Canada to reach me?"

"My business," replied Cameron gravely, "is to return to you as representative of the Eureka Paper Company, three hundred and fifty thousand dollars, which amount was paid over to me by Mr. Orcutt, and which represents the initial payment of ten percent of the purchase price of certain pulp-wood lands described in the accompanying contract of sale."

"Return the money!" cried Wentworth. "What do you mean?"

"Simply, that the deal is off. Or, rather, no valid transaction was ever consummated."

Every particle of color faded from the engineer's face at the words. As he glanced wildly about him his eye caught a twinkle in the eyes of McNabb. The color flooded his face in a surge of red, and his eyes seemed to bulge with rage as he groped for words. "It's a damned lie!" he cried. "A trick of McNabb's!" He turned upon the older man: "I thought you took your defeat too easy, but you'll find you can't put anything over on me! The deal stands—and we'll fight you to the last court! If you've found some petty technicality in the contract, you better forget it. We've gone ahead in good faith and spent a million. We can employ as good lawyers as you can, and the courts won't stand for any quibbling! It's a case for the equity courts."

Cameron smiled grimly. "I am a lawyer, and as such you will permit the smile at your mention of the equity court. You would not be allowed to enter its doors. For its first precept is: He who comes into equity must come with clean hands. Are your hands clean? I think not—neither your hands nor Orcutt's. But, the matter will never reach the courts. There is no question of a technical error in the contract, because there is no contract. The instrument I drew, and which was signed by Orcutt and myself, has no legal existence. No valid contract could have been drawn relative to the disposal of those lands until the options held by Mr. McNabb had expired—"

"But they had expired!" cried Wentworth. "They expired at twelve o'clock, noon, of July first, and the contract was not signed until two or three minutes after twelve."

"By Orcutt's watch," retorted Cameron. "And Orcutt's watch was an hour faster than official time. I had no reason to suppose his watch was wrong, and believed the time had expired, until I was confronted, after your departure, by the accredited representative of McNabb. I was dumbfounded until I established the fact that he was within his rights in tendering payment and closing the transaction for his principal. Then there was no course open to me but to accept McNabb's money and conclude the transfer to him. Murchison, here, is a witness, that the facts are as I have stated them."

Wentworth's eyes flew to the face of the factor, who nodded emphatically. Again the color left his face. "It's a damned trick!" he muttered. "Why didn't you notify us at once, instead of waiting nearly three weeks and allowing us to spend more than a million dollars?"

"Orcutt told me he would return to the post in two days. I waited, and when a week went by I used every means in my power to reach him. I followed him by train. I learned his address and wired the facts to his bank. The fault is his own. I am sorry you have lost so heavily—"

"It isn't my money," Wentworth cried savagely. Then he suddenly paused, and for upwards of thirty seconds the room was in dead silence. When he spoke again, it was in a voice palpably held in control.

"I guess you have got us," he said. "There seems to be nothing for me to do but accept the money." He held out his hand as Cameron slowly counted out the big bills. Then without recounting, Wentworth thrust them into his pocket, and with quick, nervous strokes of his pen signed the receipt which Cameron placed before him. Then in a voice trembling with suppressed rage he faced McNabb. "Damn you!" he cried. "I thought—Orcutt said you were beginning to slip!"

"Well, maybe he's right," admitted McNabb, and the engineer saw that his lips twitched at the corners.

"Who was your representative?" he demanded abruptly. "And, how did it come that he arrived just in the nick of time?"

"Why, his name is Sven Larsen. He's Murchison's clerk," answered the Scot. "And he was here all the time."

"Sven Larsen!" yelled Wentworth. "That half-wit! Why, he hasn't got sense enough to come in out of the rain!"

"Maybe ye're right," admitted McNabb, "but that isn't what I hired him to do."

With an oath, Wentworth pushed past Cameron and started for the door to find himself suddenly face to face with Sven Larsen. "Get out of my way, damn you!" he cried. "Go up in the loft and wallow in your stinking furs!"

"Furs!" repeated the clerk dully, but without giving an inch. "Oh, yes, furs." He was looking Wentworth squarely in the eyes with a heavy stare. "Some fur is good, and some is bad. A Russian sable is better than a baum marten." At the words, Jean McNabb, who had been a silent but fascinated listener to all that transpired, leaned swiftly forward, her eyes staring into the uncouth face of the speaker, who continued, "And when the coat is dark, and of matched skins, it is very much better than any baum marten. And when one receives the sable coat on a winter's night from the hands of a beautiful Russian princess whom one is helping to escape through a roaring blizzard in a motor car—or was it a sleigh?"

"Stop, damn you!" In the lamp-light the on-lookers saw that the face of the engineer had gone livid. His words came thickly. "You fool! Are you crazy? Have you forgotten Pollak, and what happened in the shop of Levinski, the furrier? Where is Pollak?"

A slow grin overspread the face of Sven Larsen. "I invented Pollak to cover a mistake I made. There never was any Pollak, Wentworth, but there is a Russian sable coat. The coat is in your trunk in the cabin. It is the coat you stole from Miss McNabb on the night of the Campbell dinner."

"Oskar!" cried Jean, leaping from her chair at the moment that Wentworth hurled himself upon Hedin. Her cry was drowned in the swift impact of bodies and the sound of blows, and grunts, and heavy breathing. McNabb and Cameron drew back and the bodies, locked in a clench, toppled to the floor, overturning a chair.

"Oh, stop them! Stop them!" shrieked the girl. "He'll kill him!"

"Who'll kill who?" grinned McNabb, holding her back with one hand, without taking his eyes from the struggling, fighting figures that writhed almost at his feet, overturning boxes and bales in their struggles.

"He'll kill Oskar! He's bigger—"

"Not by a damn sight, he won't!" roared McNabb. "Look at um! Look at um! Oskar's on top! Give him hell, lad!"

Jean had ceased her protest, and to her own intense surprise she found herself leaning forward, watching every move. She cried out with pain when Wentworth's fist brought the blood from Oskar's nose, and she applauded when Hedin's last three blows landed with vicious thuds against the engineer's upturned chin.

Hedin rose to his feet and held the handkerchief to his bleeding nose. McNabb's hand gripped his shoulder. "Ye done fine, lad! Ye done fine!" he exclaimed.

Dropping to his knees, Hedin slipped his hand into the unconscious man's pocket and withdrew a key which he tossed to one of the Company Indians who had come running in at the sound of battle. "Here, Joe Irish," he said, "go to the cabin and unlock the trunk that is there and bring back the coat of fur."

A few moments later Hedin handed the garment to McNabb. "Here is your missing coat," he said, as Jean threw her arm about his shoulder.

"Oskar, dear—" she whispered, and the next moment Hedin's arms were about her and she could feel the wild pounding of his heart against her breast.

There was a movement on the floor near their feet, and releasing the girl Hedin reached swiftly down. McNabb's hand stayed him before he could seize hold of Wentworth, who was crawling toward the door.

"Let him go, lad," advised the old man. "We've got the coat. An'—an'—we're all happy!"

"But the money? He's got the three hundred and fifty thousand!" cried Hedin.

McNabb grinned. "Suppose we just let Orcutt worry about that," he said.

"I told you Oskar was innocent!" cried Jean triumphantly, as the door closed behind the slinking form of Wentworth. "I told you so from the first! I just knew he never took that coat!"

McNabb's eyes were twinkling. "I knew it, too, lass," he answered. "That's why I bailed him out an' sent him up here with two hundred an' fifty thousand dollars in negotiable paper in his pocket to close this deal for me."

"And you knew all the time," cried the girl, staring at her father in amazement, "when Orcutt was gloating over you back there, that you, and not he, owned the timber? And you let him go on and humiliate you to your face!"

"Sure I did," grinned McNabb. "He was havin' the time of his life, an' I hated to spoil it. An' besides, while he was talkin', truck after truck was rollin' off down the tote-road haulin' material to my mill site that I'll buy in at ten cents on the dollar. Orcutt'll pay for his fun!"

"But—your face—when he told you that you had lost the timber! It positively went gray!"

"Poker face," laughed McNabb. "But run along now—the two of ye. It's many a long day since Dugald an' I have had a powwow with our feet cocked up on bales of Injun goods." As the two walked arm in arm toward the door, McNabb called to the girl, "Here, lass, take your coat!" He tossed the Russian sable which the girl caught with a glad cry. "Ye'll be needin' it up here agin winter comes."

"Winter! Up here! What do you mean?"

"Oskar says he isn't goin' back to Terrace City," he explained. "Except maybe for the weddin'. The North has got into his blood, an' the McNabb Paper Company needs a competent manager."

XXV

When Wentworth left the trading room he went straight to his cabin, and disregarding his open trunk, he lifted a pack-sack from the floor and swung it to his shoulders. It was the pack he had deposited there scarcely an hour before when he had trailed in from the mill site, and he knew that it contained three or four days' supply of rations.

On the Shamattawa he had heard from a truck driver that an old man and a girl had started for Gods Lake post, and he instantly recognized McNabb and Jean from the man's description. Thereupon he made up a pack and headed for the post for the sole purpose of baiting the two, and of flaunting his prowess as a financier in their faces.

An angry flush flooded his face as he realized how completely the tables had turned. Then the flush gave place to a crafty smile, as he remembered the bills in his pocket. "McNabb's money, or Orcutt's," he muttered under his breath, "it's all the same to me. Three hundred and fifty thousand is more money than I ever expected to handle. And now for the get-away."

Closing the door behind him he struck across the clearing toward the northeast. At the end of the bush he paused. "Hell!" he growled. "I can't hit for the railway. Cameron said he had wired Orcutt at the bank, and I might meet him coming in." For some time he stood irresolute. "There's a way out straight south," he speculated, "about three hundred miles, and a good share of it water trail. I'll be all right if I can pick up a canoe, and I can get grub of the Indians." Skirting the clearing, he entered the bush and came out on the shore of the lake at some distance below the landing, where several canoes had been beached for the night. Stooping, he righted one, and as he straightened up he found himself face to face with Corporal Downey of the Mounted. For a moment the two stood regarding each other in silence, while through Wentworth's brain flashed a mighty fear. Had McNabb changed his mind and sent Downey to arrest him for the theft of the coat? He thought of Orcutt's big bills in his pocket, and his blood seemed to turn to water within him. Then suddenly he remembered that for the present, at least, he held those bills under color of authority. In the deep twilight that is the summer midnight of the North he searched the officer's face. Damn the man! Why didn't he say something? Why did he always force another to open a conversation? Wentworth cleared his throat.

"Hello, *Corporal*," he said sourly. "Aren't you out pretty late?"

"Not any later than you are, *Captain*. An' I'm headed in. Put over any more big deals lately?"

"What do you mean?"

"Oh, I run onto Cameron about a week back. He was huntin' you or Orcutt. He told me how you beat old John McNabb out of his pulp-wood—almost. You ought to be ashamed—a couple of up-to-date financiers like you two, pickin' on an' old man that's just dodderin' around in his second childhood."

Wentworth flushed hot at the grin that accompanied the words.

"To hell with McNabb—and you, too!" he cried angrily, and carrying the canoe into the water, he placed his pack in it. When he returned for a paddle, Downey was gone, and stepping into the canoe, he pushed it out into the lake. "Of course, he'd have to show up, damn him!" he muttered as he propelled the light craft southward with swift strokes of the paddle. "And now if Orcutt should show up within the next day or two, Downey will know just where to follow, and even with a two days' start, I doubt if I could keep ahead of him. They say he's a devil on the trail. But I'll fool him. I'll leave the canoe at the end of the lake, and instead of striking on down the river I'll hit out overland. Once I get to the railway, they can all go to hell!"

The mistake Wentworth made on the trail when he first came into the North was not so much the insisting upon bringing in his trunk, nor his refusal to carry a pack; it was in striking Alex Thumb with the dog-whip when he refused to pull the outfit in the face of a blizzard. Thumb's reputation as a "bad Injun" was well founded. The son of a hot-tempered French trader and a Cree mother, his early life had been a succession of merciless beatings. At the age of fourteen he killed his father with a blow from an ice chisel, and thereafter served ten years of an indeterminate sentence, during the course of which the unmerciful beatings were administered for each infraction of reformatory rules, until in his heart was born a sullen hatred of all white men and an abysmal hatred of the lash. When Wentworth struck, his doom was sealed, but as Murchison said, Alex Thumb was canny. He had no mind to serve another term in prison.

All through the spring and summer he trailed the engineer, waiting with the patience that is the heritage of the wilderness dweller for the time and the place to strike and avoid suspicion. And as time drew on the half-breed's hatred against all white men seemed to concentrate into a mighty rage against this one white man. There had been times when he could have killed him from afar. More than once on the trail Wentworth unconsciously stood with the sights of Alex Thumb's rifle trained upon his head, or his heart. But such was his hatred that Thumb always stayed the finger that crooked upon the trigger—and bided his time.

Thus it was that half an hour after Wentworth pushed out into the lake another canoe shot out from the shore and fell in behind, its lone occupant, paddling noiselessly, easily kept just within sight of the fleeing man. When daylight broadened Wentworth landed upon a sandy point and ate breakfast. Upon another point, a mile to the rear, Alex Thumb lay on his belly and chewed jerked meat as his smouldering black eyes regarded gloatingly the man in the distance.

Gods Lake is nearly fifty miles in its north and south reach, and all day Wentworth paddled southward, holding well to the western shore.

At noon he rested for an hour and ate luncheon, his eyes now and then scanning the back reach of the lake. But he saw nothing, and from an aspen thicket scarce half a mile away Alex Thumb watched in silence.

As the afternoon wore to a closer the half-breed drew nearer. The shadows of the bordering balsams were long on the water when Wentworth first caught sight of the pursuing canoe. His first thought was that Orcutt had arrived at the post and that Downey had taken the trail. He ceased paddling for a moment and his light canoe swung into the trough of the waves and rocked crankily.

The other canoe was only a half mile behind, and Wentworth saw with relief that its occupant was not Downey. Some Indian fishing, he thought, and resumed his paddling. The south shore was only an hour away now, and tired as he was, he redoubled his efforts.

Farther on he looked back again. The canoe still followed. Surely no Indian would set his nets so far from his camp. Yet the man was an Indian. He had drawn closer and Wentworth could distinguish the short, jabbing strokes of the paddle.

Another quarter of an hour and Wentworth looked again—and as he looked, the blood seemed to freeze in his veins. The pursuing canoe was close now, and he was staring straight into the eyes of Alex Thumb. The half-breed was smiling—a curious, twisted smile that was the very embodiment of savage hate. Wentworth's muscles felt weak, and it was with difficulty that he drove them to the task of forcing the canoe out of the trough of the waves. Mechanically he paddled with his eyes fixed on the ever nearing south shore. He was very tired. He would soon make land now. But when he did make land—what then? He cursed himself for going unarmed. He could hear the slop of the waves on Thumb's canoe. He turned his head and saw that the man was only two lengths behind him. What would he do? With the mechanical swing of his arms the words of Murchison and Downey repeated themselves in his brain. "Serving with the devils in hell; serving with the devils in hell," with a certain monotonous rhythm the words kept repeating themselves through his brain. Why had he ever come North? Why hadn't he told McNabb that he would have nothing to do with his pulp-wood? The half-breed's canoe was alongside, but its occupant did not speak. He merely jabbed at the waves with his paddle and looked with that devilish twisted smile.

Wentworth hardly knew when his canoe grated upon the gravel. Stiffly he half walked, half crawled to the bow and lifted out his pack. Alex Thumb stood upon the gravel and smiled.

"What do you want?" faltered Wentworth, his voice breaking nervously.

The half-breed shrugged. "You no lak no pardner on de trail?" he asked.

"Where are you going?"

Thumb pointed vaguely toward the south. "Me—I'm lak de pardner on de trail."

"Look here," cried Wentworth suddenly. "Do you want money? More money than you ever saw before?"

The breed shook his head. "No. De money can't buy w'at I wan'."

"What do you want?"

Again came the twisted smile. "Mebbe-so we eat de suppaire firs'. I got som' feesh. We buil' de fire an' cook 'um."

The meal was eaten in silence, and during its progress Wentworth in a measure recovered his nerve.

"You haven't told me yet what you want," he suggested when they had lighted their pipes and thrown on an armful of greens for a smudge.

Between the narrowed lids the black eyes seemed to smoulder as they fixed upon the face of the white man. "I wan' you heart," he said, casually. "Red in my han's I wan' it, an' squeeze de blood out, an' watch it splash on de rocks. Mebbe-so I'm eat a piece dat heart, an' feed de res' to my dog."

Wentworth's pipe dropped to the gravel and lay there. He uttered no sound. The wind had died down and save for the droning hum of a billion mosquitoes the silence was absolute. A thin column of smoke streamed from the bowl of the neglected pipe. In profound fascination Wentworth watched it flow smoothly upward. An imperceptible air current set the column swaying and wavering, and a light puff of breeze dispersed it in a swirl of heavy yellow smoke from the smudge. Dully, impersonally, he sensed that the half-breed had just told him that he would squeeze the red blood from his heart and watch it splash upon the rocks. His eyes rested upon the rocks rimmed up by the ice above the gravelly beach. The blood would splash there, and there, and those other rocks would be spattered with tiny drops of it— his blood, the blood from his own heart which Alex Thumb would squeeze dry, as one would wring water from a sponge. He wondered that he felt no sense of fear. He believed that Alex Thumb would do that, yet it was a matter that seemed not of any importance. He raised his eyes and encountered the malevolent glare of the breed. The black eyes seemed to glow with an inner lustre, like the smoulder of banked fires.

With a start he seemed to have returned from some far place. The words of Corporal Downey flittered through his brain: "You'll be servin' with the devils in hell if you don't quit makin' enemies of men like Alex Thumb." And there was Alex Thumb regarding him through narrowed smouldering eyes across the little fire. Alex Thumb would kill him! Would kill *him*—Ross Wentworth! The whole thing was preposterous. If the man had really meant to kill him he would have done it before this. He wouldn't dare; there were the Mounted. Other words of Downey came to him, "If he does kill you, I'll get him." So there was a possibility that the man would kill him. Why not? Who would ever know? They would think he disappeared with Orcutt's money—would even institute a world-wide search from him—but not in the bush. Thought of the money nerved him to speak.

"How much will you take to get into your canoe and paddle back the way you came?" he asked.

The breed laughed. "Wen I'm keel you I'm got you money, anyway. But I'm ain' wan' so mooch de money. I'm wan' you heart." A dangerous glitter supplanted the smouldering glow of the black eyes. "Me—I'm stay ten year in de prison, for 'cause I'm keel my own fadder, an' dat dam' good t'ing. For why I'm keel heem? 'Cause he whip me wit' de dog-whip. In de prison de guards whip me mor' as wan t'ousan' tam. In de night w'en I ain' can sleep 'cause my back hurt so bad from de whip, I'm lay in de dark an' keel dem all. Every wan I ha' keel wan hondre tam dere in de dark w'en I lay an' t'ink 'bout it. An' I know how I'm goin' do dat. Den you hit me wit de whip on de trail. All right. I'm ain' kin keel de guards. I keel you here in de bush; I shoot you in de head, an' I'm cut de heart out before he quit jumpin'."

Wentworth moistened his lips with his tongue. "Downey will take you in, if you do. And they'll hang you—choke you to death with a rope."

"No. Downey ain' kin fin'. I'm bur' you in de bush—all but de heart. I'm keep de heart all tam."

"Good God, man, you couldn't kill me like that—in cold blood!" Beyond the fire the half-breed laughed, a dry evil laugh that held nothing of mirth. With a scream of terror Wentworth leaped to his feet and crashed into the bush.

Beside the fire Alex Thumb laughed—and spread his blankets for the night.

Four hours later the breed wriggled from his blanket and lighted the fire. While the water heated for his tea, he carried the two canoes back into the scrub and cached them, together with the two packs. He swallowed his breakfast and picking up his rifle walked slowly into the bush, his eyes on the ground. A mile away the lips twisted into their sardonic grin as he noted where the fleeing man had floundered through a muskeg, the flattened grass telling of his frequent falls. In a balsam thicket he lifted a scrap of cloth from a protruding limb, and again he smiled. Where Wentworth forded a waist-deep stream he had lain down to rest on the sand of the opposite bank. The trail started toward the south. By midforenoon Thumb noted with a grin that he was traveling due east.

At noon he overtook Wentworth, mired to the middle in a marl bed, supporting himself on a half sunken spruce.

Laying aside his rifle, the breed cut a pole with his belt ax and after some difficulty succeeded in dragging the engineer to solid ground. Wentworth was muttering and mumbling about a Russian sable coat, and Thumb had to support him as he bound him to a spruce tree.

On the edge of the lake Corporal Downey picked up the trail. He located the cached canoes, and returning to the fire, he reached down and picked Wentworth's pipe from the gravel. "It's Thumb, all right," he said, as he stood holding the pipe. "I know his canoe. They were both here at the same time. I don't savvy that, because Wentworth left first. Thumb's trail is only three hours old. Maybe—if I hurry—"

From far to the southeastward came the sound of a shot.

Downey straightened, and for the space of minutes stood tense as a pointer. The sound was not repeated—and swiftly the officer of the Mounted sped through the bush.

AN EPILOGUE

Two days later, into the trading room of the Hudson's Bay Company's post on God's Lake, burst Orcutt, white of face, shaken of nerves, and with his disheveled garments bespeaking a frenzied dash through the timber.

"What's the meaning of this?" he cried, holding out a telegram.

McNabb reached for the message and read it. "It means just what it says," he answered. "Cameron has stated it plain."

"But where is Cameron? Where is the three hundred and fifty thousand I paid him? Where is Wentworth?"

"Cameron is not here. He left after turning over your money to Wentworth. He said he held a paper that constituted Wentworth your legal representative."

"But—where is Wentworth?" gasped Orcutt.

"He left the night he got the money—a week ago to-night, wasn't it, Dugald?"

"Good God!" The words were a groan. "I'm ruined. Ruined, I tell you! There's just one chance. John, the material that's on your mill site. Will you take it over?"

"Sure, I'll take it," answered McNabb. "On the same terms you offered for my tote-road. Ten cents on the dollar, wasn't it, Orcutt?"

"But, man, you don't understand!"

"I understand that the shoe is on the other foot," answered McNabb, coldly. "Listen to me, Orcutt; by your own admission you've been trying for more than twenty years to ruin me. I've let you go, never turning out of my way to injure you. I'm not turning out of my way now. If you're squeezed it is because of your own deeds—not mine."

"Squeezed!" sobbed the banker hysterically. "I'm ruined! It means the bank—my home—everything! It means—more. I was so sure—I—I'm into the bank's money for thousands! It means—the penitentiary!"

McNabb looked at the cringing man, whose knees seemed to sag beneath the weight of his woe. Coldly his eyes traveled the length of him: "Maybe ye're right," he said, and his words cut icy cold. Then, deliberately he turned his back upon the man and strode through the door.

Upon that same day, also came Corporal Downey, of the Royal North West Mounted Police, and in his custody he held a man. The man was the half-breed Alex Thumb.

"We've got the goods on him this time," Downey told the factor. "And a damned peculiar case. I picked him up a few miles south of the lake. I heard a shot, and an hour later I located him and crept up through the brush. He had just finished burying Wentworth's body all but the heart—that was dryin' on a little stick beside the fire. There was an

empty shell in his rifle. But—what I can't make out is this."
He paused and withdrew from his pocket a small tin box, and
opening it, disclosed a handful of ashes and the half of a
United States gold certificate for ten thousand dollars. "He
was holdin' it over a little fire," explained the officer. "I
located him by the smoke smell. I covered him, and he
dropped this last fragment to throw up his hands. It's money.
I didn't know they made 'em so big. But why in hell should
he burn it?"

Murchison examined the fragment with its burned edge.
"Alex Thumb was canny," he muttered. "The bills was too
big. He didn't dare to spend 'em."

THE END

Choose from Thousands of 1stWorldLibrary Classics By

A. M. Barnard
Ada Leverson
Adolphus William Ward
Aesop
Agatha Christie
Alexander Aaronsohn
Alexander Kielland
Alexandre Dumas
Alfred Gatty
Alfred Ollivant
Alice Duer Miller
Alice Turner Curtis
Alice Dunbar
Allen Chapman
Alleyne Ireland
Ambrose Bierce
Amelia E. Barr
Amory H. Bradford
Andrew Lang
Andrew McFarland Davis
Andy Adams
Angela Brazil
Anna Alice Chapin
Anna Sewell
Annie Besant
Annie Hamilton Donnell
Annie Payson Call
Annie Roe Carr
Annonaymous
Anton Chekhov
Archibald Lee Fletcher
Arnold Bennett
Arthur C. Benson
Arthur Conan Doyle
Arthur M. Winfield
Arthur Ransome
Arthur Schnitzler
Arthur Train
Atticus
B.H. Baden-Powell
B. M. Bower
B. C. Chatterjee
Baroness Emmuska Orczy
Baroness Orczy
Basil King
Bayard Taylor
Ben Macomber
Bertha Muzzy Bower
Bjornstjerne Bjornson

Booth Tarkington
Boyd Cable
Bram Stoker
C. Collodi
C. E. Orr
C. M. Ingleby
Carolyn Wells
Catherine Parr Traill
Charles A. Eastman
Charles Amory Beach
Charles Dickens
Charles Dudley Warner
Charles Farrar Browne
Charles Ives
Charles Kingsley
Charles Klein
Charles Hanson Towne
Charles Lathrop Pack
Charles Romyn Dake
Charles Whibley
Charles Willing Beale
Charlotte M. Braeme
Charlotte M. Yonge
Charlotte Perkins Stetson
Clair W. Hayes
Clarence Day Jr.
Clarence E. Mulford
Clemence Housman
Confucius
Coningsby Dawson
Cornelis DeWitt Wilcox
Cyril Burleigh
D. H. Lawrence
Daniel Defoe
David Garnett
Dinah Craik
Don Carlos Janes
Donald Keyhoe
Dorothy Kilner
Dougan Clark
Douglas Fairbanks
E. Nesbit
E. P. Roe
E. Phillips Oppenheim
E. S. Brooks
Earl Barnes
Edgar Rice Burroughs
Edith Van Dyne
Edith Wharton

Edward Everett Hale
Edward J. O'Biren
Edward S. Ellis
Edwin L. Arnold
Eleanor Atkins
Eleanor Hallowell Abbott
Eliot Gregory
Elizabeth Gaskell
Elizabeth McCracken
Elizabeth Von Arnim
Ellem Key
Emerson Hough
Emilie F. Carlen
Emily Bronte
Emily Dickinson
Enid Bagnold
Enilor Macartney Lane
Erasmus W. Jones
Ernie Howard Pie
Ethel May Dell
Ethel Turner
Ethel Watts Mumford
Eugene Sue
Eugenie Foa
Eugene Wood
Eustace Hale Ball
Evelyn Everett-green
Everard Cotes
F. H. Cheley
F. J. Cross
F. Marion Crawford
Fannie E. Newberry
Federick Austin Ogg
Ferdinand Ossendowski
Fergus Hume
Florence A. Kilpatrick
Fremont B. Deering
Francis Bacon
Francis Darwin
Frances Hodgson Burnett
Frances Parkinson Keyes
Frank Gee Patchin
Frank Harris
Frank Jewett Mather
Frank L. Packard
Frank V. Webster
Frederic Stewart Isham
Frederick Trevor Hill
Frederick Winslow Taylor

Friedrich Kerst
Friedrich Nietzsche
Fyodor Dostoyevsky
G.A. Henty
G.K. Chesterton
Gabrielle E. Jackson
Garrett P. Serviss
Gaston Leroux
George A. Warren
George Ade
Geroge Bernard Shaw
George Cary Eggleston
George Durston
George Ebers
George Eliot
George Gissing
George MacDonald
George Meredith
George Orwell
George Sylvester Viereck
George Tucker
George W. Cable
George Wharton James
Gertrude Atherton
Gordon Casserly
Grace E. King
Grace Gallatin
Grace Greenwood
Grant Allen
Guillermo A. Sherwell
Gulielma Zollinger
Gustav Flaubert
H. A. Cody
H. B. Irving
H.C. Bailey
H. G. Wells
H. H. Munro
H. Irving Hancock
H. R. Naylor
H. Rider Haggard
H. W. C. Davis
Haldeman Julius
Hall Caine
Hamilton Wright Mabie
Hans Christian Andersen
Harold Avery
Harold McGrath
Harriet Beecher Stowe
Harry Castlemon
Harry Coghill
Harry Houidini

Hayden Carruth
Helent Hunt Jackson
Helen Nicolay
Hendrik Conscience
Hendy David Thoreau
Henri Barbusse
Henrik Ibsen
Henry Adams
Henry Ford
Henry Frost
Henry James
Henry Jones Ford
Henry Seton Merriman
Henry W Longfellow
Herbert A. Giles
Herbert Carter
Herbert N. Casson
Herman Hesse
Hildegard G. Frey
Homer
Honore De Balzac
Horace B. Day
Horace Walpole
Horatio Alger Jr.
Howard Pyle
Howard R. Garis
Hugh Lofting
Hugh Walpole
Humphry Ward
Ian Maclaren
Inez Haynes Gillmore
Irving Bacheller
Isabel Cecilia Williams
Isabel Hornibrook
Israel Abrahams
Ivan Turgenev
J.G.Austin
J. Henri Fabre
J. M. Barrie
J. M. Walsh
J. Macdonald Oxley
J. R. Miller
J. S. Fletcher
J. S. Knowles
J. Storer Clouston
J. W. Duffield
Jack London
Jacob Abbott
James Allen
James Andrews
James Baldwin

James Branch Cabell
James DeMille
James Joyce
James Lane Allen
James Lane Allen
James Oliver Curwood
James Oppenheim
James Otis
James R. Driscoll
Jane Abbott
Jane Austen
Jane L. Stewart
Janet Aldridge
Jens Peter Jacobsen
Jerome K. Jerome
Jessie Graham Flower
John Buchan
John Burroughs
John Cournos
John F. Kennedy
John Gay
John Glasworthy
John Habberton
John Joy Bell
John Kendrick Bangs
John Milton
John Philip Sousa
John Taintor Foote
Jonas Lauritz Idemil Lie
Jonathan Swift
Joseph A. Altsheler
Joseph Carey
Joseph Conrad
Joseph E. Badger Jr
Joseph Hergesheimer
Joseph Jacobs
Jules Vernes
Julian Hawthrone
Julie A Lippmann
Justin Huntly McCarthy
Kakuzo Okakura
Karle Wilson Baker
Kate Chopin
Kenneth Grahame
Kenneth McGaffey
Kate Langley Bosher
Kate Langley Bosher
Katherine Cecil Thurston
Katherine Stokes
L. A. Abbot
L. T. Meade

L. Frank Baum
Latta Griswold
Laura Dent Crane
Laura Lee Hope
Laurence Housman
Lawrence Beasley
Leo Tolstoy
Leonid Andreyev
Lewis Carroll
Lewis Sperry Chafer
Lilian Bell
Lloyd Osbourne
Louis Hughes
Louis Joseph Vance
Louis Tracy
Louisa May Alcott
Lucy Fitch Perkins
Lucy Maud Montgomery
Luther Benson
Lydia Miller Middleton
Lyndon Orr
M. Corvus
M. H. Adams
Margaret E. Sangster
Margret Howth
Margaret Vandercook
Margaret W. Hungerford
Margret Penrose
Maria Edgeworth
Maria Thompson Daviess
Mariano Azuela
Marion Polk Angellotti
Mark Overton
Mark Twain
Mary Austin
Mary Catherine Crowley
Mary Cole
Mary Hastings Bradley
Mary Roberts Rinehart
Mary Rowlandson
M. Wollstonecraft Shelley
Maud Lindsay
Max Beerbohm
Myra Kelly
Nathaniel Hawthrone
Nicolo Machiavelli
O. F. Walton
Oscar Wilde

Owen Johnson
P.G. Wodehouse
Paul and Mabel Thorne
Paul G. Tomlinson
Paul Severing
Percy Brebner
Percy Keese Fitzhugh
Peter B. Kyne
Plato
Quincy Allen
R. Derby Holmes
R. L. Stevenson
R. S. Ball
Rabindranath Tagore
Rahul Alvares
Ralph Bonehill
Ralph Henry Barbour
Ralph Victor
Ralph Waldo Emmerson
Rene Descartes
Ray Cummings
Rex Beach
Rex E. Beach
Richard Harding Davis
Richard Jefferies
Richard Le Gallienne
Robert Barr
Robert Frost
Robert Gordon Anderson
Robert L. Drake
Robert Lansing
Robert Lynd
Robert Michael Ballantyne
Robert W. Chambers
Rosa Nouchette Carey
Rudyard Kipling
Saint Augustine
Samuel B. Allison
Samuel Hopkins Adams
Sarah Bernhardt
Sarah C. Hallowell
Selma Lagerlof
Sherwood Anderson
Sigmund Freud
Standish O'Grady
Stanley Weyman
Stella Benson
Stella M. Francis

Stephen Crane
Stewart Edward White
Stijn Streuvels
Swami Abhedananda
Swami Parmananda
T. S. Ackland
T. S. Arthur
The Princess Der Ling
Thomas A. Janvier
Thomas A Kempis
Thomas Anderton
Thomas Bailey Aldrich
Thomas Bulfinch
Thomas De Quincey
Thomas Dixon
Thomas H. Huxley
Thomas Hardy
Thomas More
Thornton W. Burgess
U. S. Grant
Upton Sinclair
Valentine Williams
Various Authors
Vaughan Kester
Victor Appleton
Victor G. Durham
Victoria Cross
Virginia Woolf
Wadsworth Camp
Walter Camp
Walter Scott
Washington Irving
Wilbur Lawton
Wilkie Collins
Willa Cather
Willard F. Baker
William Dean Howells
William le Queux
W. Makepeace Thackeray
William W. Walter
William Shakespeare
Winston Churchill
Yei Theodora Ozaki
Yogi Ramacharaka
Young E. Allison
Zane Grey